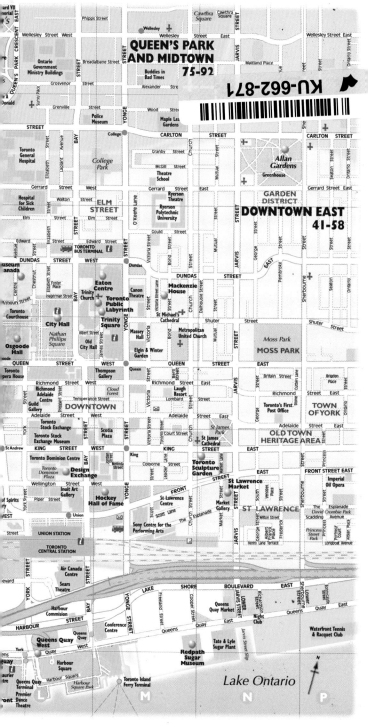

CITYPACK TOP 25
Toronto

ARILYN WOOD
DITIONAL WRITING BY PENNY PHENIX

have any comments
gestions for this guide
n contact the editor at
ick@theAA.com

AA Publishing
Find out more about AA Publishing and the wide
range of services the AA provides by visiting our
website at www.theAA.com/travel

How to Use This Book

KEY TO SYMBOLS

➕ Map reference to the accompanying fold-out map

✉ Address

☎ Telephone number

🕐 Opening/closing times

🍴 Restaurant or café

🚆 Nearest rail station

🚇 Nearest subway (Metro) station

🚌 Nearest bus route

⛴ Nearest riverboat or ferry stop

♿ Facilities for visitors with disabilities

❓ Other practical information

▷ Further information

ℹ Tourist information

✋ Admission charges: Expensive (more than $12), Moderate ($7–$12), and Inexpensive ($6 or less)

★ Major Sight   ★ Minor Sight

👣 Walks   🚐 Excursions

🏬 Shops

🎵 Entertainment and Nightlife

🍴 Restaurants

This guide is divided into four sections

• Essential Toronto: An introduction to the city and tips on making the most of your stay.
• Toronto by Area: We've broken the city into five areas, and recommended the best sights, shops, entertainment venues, nightlife and restaurants in each one. Suggested walks help you to explore on foot.
• Where to Stay: The best hotels, whether you're looking for luxury, budget or something in between.
• Need to Know: The info you need to make your trip run smoothly, including getting about by public transport, weather tips, emergency phone numbers and useful websites.

Navigation In the Toronto by Area chapter, we've given each area its own color, which is also used on the locator maps throughout the book and the map on the inside front cover.

Maps The fold-out map accompanying this book is a comprehensive street plan of Toronto. The grid on this fold-out map is the same as the grid on the locator maps within the book. We've given grid references within the book for each sight and listing.

Contents

CONTENTS

Introducing Toronto

Has anyone ever tried to tell you that Canada is dull? Let them visit Toronto, then see what they've got to say. Among the top entertainment capitals on the planet, it is vibrant, vivacious, stunningly good looking… a definite A-list of a destination.

The A-list come here, too, from all over the world, especially for the film festival. Ottawa may be the nation's capital, but Toronto is where it's at, and neither the soaring cost of real estate nor the summer smog that occasionally covers downtown has stopped it becoming North America's fifth-largest city and Canada's premier tourist destination.

Immigrants still arrive at the rate of around 100,000 a year, and their diversity has made Toronto one of the most multicultural cities in the world. This is no melting pot, though; it's a honeycomb of colorful neighborhoods offering a world of atmospheres, from exotic Asian enclaves to leafy streets with all the laid-back ambience of old Europe. The tensions that mar many immigrant-heavy cities are conspicuously absent and though there are a few no-go areas, after dark Toronto is generally safe and friendly. The city's motto says it all: Diversity our Strength.

An air of enthusiasm pervades the city. Downtown is populated by a mix of dynamic businesspeople and laid-back individals, but they all share a common desire for their city to be best (and preferably first) at everything. This extends to their "green" credentials, the size and quality of their museums and galleries, the plethora of home-grown talent in the arts and entertainment world, and the achievements of their scientists and academics.

Toronto has many attractions, but to get a real feel for the city it's just as important simply to hang out on a restaurant patio, on the lakeshore, or at one of the hundreds of festivals or free concerts.

Facts + Figures

- Toronto is on the same latitude as the French Riviera.
- Nearly half of Toronto's 2.5 million population were born outside of Canada.
- Toronto has more than 840km (522 miles) of cycling trails.

INSIDER INFORMATION

There's nothing like visiting a city with someone who knows their way around, but if you don't have a friend in Toronto, don't despair. The TAP into TO! scheme provides (for free) a knowledgeable local to guide you around and share some of their own city secrets. Call 416/338-2786 for information.

A RECORD LOST

For more than 30 years Toronto's CN Tower ruled supreme as the tallest free-standing building in the world, but in 2007 it was knocked into second place by a Dubai hotel (the Burj Dubai), still under construction and set to attain a final height of around 800m (2,624ft)–the CN Tower stands at 555.3m (1,821.4ft).

HOLLYWOOD NORTH

A huge number of movies and TV shows are shot in Toronto each year. Popular locations include the Distillery Historic District (*Chicago*, *Cinderella Man*, *The Man*) and Casa Loma, which was the interior of the X-Men's "school for gifted youngsters." Dundas Street featured in *Hairspray* and, at the time of going to press, *The Incredible Hulk* (Edward Norton, Liv Tyler) and *Repossession Mambo* (Jude Law) were in production.

A Short Stay in Toronto

DAY 1

Morning You might as well start out with a visit to the **CN Tower** (▷ 26–27) or it will constantly beckon from wherever else you are in the city. Arrive in good time for the 9am opening, and go all the way to the top for a spectacular overview of Toronto.

Mid-morning Walk west along Front Street to Spadina, then take a street-car north to Dundas to visit the spectacular **Art Gallery of Ontario** (AGO, ▷ 24–25), a showcase of both art and architecture.

Lunch Lunch at the AGO for a fine dining experience within the new Frank Gehry extension on Dundas Street. Canadian art adorns the walls and sustainable, organic Canadian produce is on the menu. For a lighter meal, the café downstairs is equally good.

Afternoon Take the streetcar back down Spadina all the way to the lakeshore, then stroll east to take the ferry to (**The Islands** ▷ 66–67). Rent a bicycle or just stroll through the parkland, relax on one of the sandy beaches and perhaps take a dip in the lake.

Dinner Dress up and head to the **Canoe Restaurant and Bar** (▷ 57; 54th Floor TDC Bank Tower, 66 Wellington Street West; tel: 416/364-0054). This is one of Canada's finest restaurants, with excellent food and superb views, so make sure you have a reservation.

Evening Take in a Broadway-style show, concert or comedy night, then join the after-theater crowd at any place in the Entertainment District that appeals. The choice there includes chic cocktail lounges, pubs, jazz clubs and dance clubs, and you can just stroll until you see (or hear) something you like.

DAY 2

Morning Pick up a typical Toronto breakfast of a peameal bacon sandwich at **St. Lawrence Market** (▷ 51) then walk west along Front Street to Union Station and take the metro up to the Museum stop to visit the **Royal Ontario Museum** (ROM, ▷ 84–85).

Mid-morning After the museum, walk north across Bloor Street to explore the many upscale stores on the leafy streets of Yorkville.

Lunch Le Paradis Restaurant (166 Bedford Road, tel: 416/921-0995; lunch served Tue–Fri only) is a chic brasserie/bistro with a good-value fixed-price lunch.

Afternoon Take the subway to Dupont, then walk up to visit **Casa Loma** (▷ 80–81). Later, make your way to Greektown and stroll along Danforth Avenue to soak up the European atmosphere of one of Toronto's most vibrant neighborhoods.

Dinner Dine at the renowned **Pan restaurant** (516 Danforth Avenue, tel: 416/466-8158), where traditional Greek dishes are on the menu and the wine list includes a worldwide selection, including Greek.

Evening Head back downtown for late-night live music at **Jeff Healey's Roadhouse** (▷ 37). The legendary guitarist sadly died in 2008, but the music continues and the line-up is great any day of the week. Or see the 10.30 show at **Second City** comedy club (▷ 38), Friday or Saturday only, both near the **Rogers Centre** (▷ 32).

Top 25

ESSENTIAL TORONTO TOP 25

►►►

Art Gallery of Ontario
▷ 24–25 One of Canada's principal art galleries, strong in Canadian art.

Bata Shoe Museum
▷ 78–79 Fascinating collection of shoes through the ages.

Black Creek Pioneer Village ▷ 96 A complete small rural community replicating Victorian Ontario.

University of Toronto
▷ 86 A venerable institution with an impressive roster of alumni.

Toronto Zoo ▷ 102 Animals from every continent roam spacious enclosures that try to re-create their natural habitats.

Toronto Islands
▷ 66–67 These peaceful islands with sandy beaches are just a short ferry ride away from downtown.

St. Lawrence Market
▷ 51 This historic market building offers a wonderful assortment of food.

Royal Ontario Museum
▷ 84–85 Canada's largest museum contains 6 million objects, including a superb collection of Chinese art.

Rogers Centre ▷ 32 The home of the Blue Jays is a superb multipurpose stadium, famous for its retractable roof.

Ontario Science Centre
▷ 100–101 Nine exhibition halls packed with interactive displays.

Ontario Place ▷ 64–65 Popular amusement park with rides, activities and entertainments.

Ontario Legislature
▷ 83 The home of the government of the province of Ontario.

8

These pages are a quick guide to the Top 25, which are described in more detail later. Here they are listed alphabetically, and the tinted background shows which area they are in.

Canada's Wonderland
▷ 98–99 Canada's premier theme park, with 200 attractions.

Casa Loma ▷ 80–81
A 17th-century fairy-tale castle built for an early-20th-century millionaire.

City Hall ▷ 44–45
Instantly recognizable, the futuristic-looking City Hall was designed in the 1960s.

The CN Tower ▷ 26–27
The ultimate symbol of Toronto, with the world's highest viewing platform.

Design Exchange
▷ 46–47 Graceful Moderne building now dedicated to Canadian design.

Distillery Historic District ▷ 48–49 Former distillery buildings now given over to culture.

Fort York ▷ 28–29
Historic spot where the city was founded in 1793.

Gardiner Museum of Ceramic Art ▷ 82
Superb museum devoted to ceramic art, from pre-Columbian to the present.

Harbourfront Centre
▷ 62–63 Docklands, now revitalized as a commercial, cultural and leisure center.

Hockey Hall of Fame
▷ 50 A shrine to Canada's sporting obsession.

Kensington Market
▷ 30 The perfect place to experience Toronto's vibrant multiculturalism.

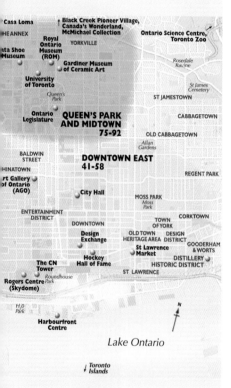

Casa Loma
THE ANNEX
Bata Shoe Museum
Royal Ontario Museum (ROM)
YORKVILLE
Gardiner Museum of Ceramic Art
University of Toronto
Queen's Park
Ontario Legislature
QUEEN'S PARK AND MIDTOWN 75-92
BALDWIN STREET
CHINATOWN
Art Gallery of Ontario (AGO)
DOWNTOWN EAST 41-58
ENTERTAINMENT DISTRICT
City Hall
DOWNTOWN
Design Exchange
The CN Tower
Hockey Hall of Fame
Rogers Centre (Skydome)
Roundhouse Park
H.O Park
Harbourfront Centre
Black Creek Pioneer Village, Canada's Wonderland, McMichael Collection
Ontario Science Centre, Toronto Zoo
Rosedale Ravine
St James Cemetery
ST JAMESTOWN
CABBAGETOWN
OLD CABBAGETOWN
Allan Gardens
REGENT PARK
MOSS PARK
Moss Park
TOWN OF YORK
CORKTOWN
OLD TOWN HERITAGE AREA
DESIGN DISTRICT
St Lawrence Market
GOODERHAM & WORTS
DISTILLERY
ST LAWRENCE
DISTILLERY HISTORIC DISTRICT
Lake Ontario
Toronto Islands
N

Museum of Contemporary Canadian Art ▷ 31 Seminal works by current Canadian artists.

McMichael Collection
▷ 97 Come here to see the influential works of the Group of Seven artists.

◀ ◀ ◀

Shopping

If you love to shop, come to Toronto with a fat wallet and a spare suitcase. The possibilities are seemingly endless, and you could shop every day for a month and still not discover all the quirky backstreet boutiques, cutting-edge products and highly individual craftworks.

From Malls to Markets

Among the particular pleasures of shopping here are the ease of getting around and the friendly staff. Add to this the delightful neighborhoods with specialty stores, the number of glittering malls and the traditional markets and you've got something really special. Even in the Financial District, the skyscraper towers often harbor one or more floors of shopping at street level.

Fashion

Most of the world's top names in fashion have found a home in Toronto, particularly on the "mink mile" (Bloor Street between Avenue Road and Yonge Street). Chanel, Max Mara, Hermès, Gucci, Prada, Versace, to name a few, have seasonal windows. Diamonds, watches and crystal sparkle at Tiffany's, Royale de Versailles, Watchcraft and Swarovski. The Canadian flagship store of Roots, a giant in casual clothing and sportswear, occupies a multilevel space and Zara, Spain's stylish budget-conscious entry in the fashion field, are here as well. Still at the heart of Bloor Street is Holt Renfrew, a three-story style emporium for men, women and the home.

St. Lawrence Market;
Chapters bookstore;
Kensington market; Yonge
Street shops (top to bottom)

A GOOD SMOKE

Canada has never severed diplomatic or trade relations with Cuba, and so just about every tobacconist in Toronto has a humidor full of Havanas—something you won't find anywhere south of the border. But if you'll be crossing into the US anytime soon, smoke those stogies in Canada: US laws embargo trade with Cuba, and trying to take goods across the border could lead to charges.

Arts and Crafts

Bloor Street is not the only game in town. On Spadina Avenue around Dundas, fur and garment manufacturers have showrooms and retail outlets. There are Pan-Asian Shopping Malls in Markham and Scarborough that will feel like something in a major city in Asia. Toronto's arts and crafts communities show their works on Queen Street West, which abounds with custom jewelers, sophisticated glass sculpture galleries and native and Inuit art. For classy antiques visit Davenport Road at Avenue.

Music

Toronto is proud of its musicians and entertainers, and the huge HMV store on Yonge Street stages live in-store performances. Most Toronto music stores dedicate shelves to Canadian-bred talent such as Bryan Adams, Avril Lavigne, Alanis Morrissette and Shania Twain.

Historic Stores

At Queen's Quay Terminal the Tilley Endurables Boutique features the Tilley Hat. Advertised as having been retrieved intact after it was eaten by an elephant, it comes with a lifetime guarantee and owner's manual. Hudson's Bay Company, a former fur trading post that's as old as Canada itself, and now known simply as The Bay, is a major store selling everything from fur items to appliances, electronics and fashions. Stores are on Queen and Bay and Bloor and Yonge, as well as in suburban shopping malls.

PICK UP A BARGAIN

There is nothing so satisfying as finding a real bargain, and the best time for this in Toronto is the first day of business after Christmas, when prices are routinely slashed by half (or more). There are sales in summer, too, roughly June through August. Year-round bargains can be found in the discount malls, such as Dixie Mall, and at Honest Ed's (581 Bloor West), a Toronto institution that's worth a visit just to see how brash and tacky it is.

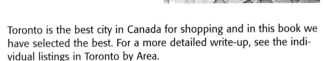

Shopping by Theme

Toronto is the best city in Canada for shopping and in this book we have selected the best. For a more detailed write-up, see the individual listings in Toronto by Area.

ANTIQUES

Abraham's (▷ 35)
Fifty One Antiques (▷ 89)
Toronto Antiques on King
  (▷ 36)

ARTS AND CRAFTS

Algonquins Sweet
  Grass Gallery (▷ 35)
Arts on King (▷ 55)
Ashley China (▷ 89)
Bounty (▷ 71)
Guild Shop (▷ 89)
International Marketplace
  (▷ 71)
Prime Gallery (▷ 36)

BOOKS AND TOYS

Book City (▷ panel, 36)
Dragon Lady Comic Shop
  (▷ 35)
Nicholas Hoare Bookshop
  (▷ panel, 36, 55)
Pages Books and
  Magazines (▷ panel,
  36)
Science City (▷ 89)
Steven Temple Books
  (▷ 36)
World's Biggest Bookstore
  (▷ 36)

CLOTHES FOR MEN

Bulloch Tailors (▷ 55)
George Bouridis (▷ 55)
GOTStyle (▷ 35)

Harry Rosen (▷ 89)
Legends of the Game
  (▷ 36)
Mountain Equipment
  Co-op (▷ 36)
Stollery's (▷ 89)
Tilley Endurables (▷ 71)

CLOTHES FOR WOMEN

Cabaret (▷ 35)
Club Monaco (▷ 35)
Freda's (▷ 35)
F/X (▷ 35)
Holt Renfrew (▷ 89)
John Fluevog (▷ 36)
Mountain Equipment
  Co-op (▷ 36)
The Rage (▷ 36)
Stollery's (▷ 89)
Tilley Endurables (▷ 71)

FOOD AND DRINK

All the Best Fine Foods
  (▷ 89)
Daniel et Daniel (▷ 55)
The Dish Cooking Studio
  (▷ 89)
Kitchen Table (▷ 71)
LCBO (▷ 71)
Ten Ren Tea (▷ 36)

JEWELRY

Corktown Design (▷ 55)
Anne Sportun Experimental
  Jewellery (▷ 35)
Silverbridge (▷ 89)

MALLS/DEPARTMENT STORES

Atrium on Bay (▷ 55)
The Bay (▷ 55)
Brookfield Place (▷ 55)
College Park (▷ 55)
Eaton Centre (▷ 55)
First Canadian Place
  (▷ 55)
Queen's Quay Terminal
  (▷ 71)

MUSIC

L'Atelier Gregorian (▷ 89)
Rhythm Corner (▷ 36)

SPORTS

Legends of the Game
  (▷ 36)
Mountain Equipment
  Co-op (▷ 36)
Wheel Excitement (▷ 71)

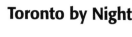

Toronto by Night

Toronto is as lively by night as it is in daylight, only just behind New York and London in the nightlife stakes. There's a theater district (▷ below) and plenty of other theaters around the city. There are several world-class concert halls, stadium rock concerts at the Rogers Centre or Molson Amphitheatre, atmospheric live venues that leave no musical stone unturned, and a huge choice of nightclubs and bars. The streets are generally safe and public transportation after dark is good.

Clubs, Clubs and More Clubs

The club-lined streets of downtown Toronto are filled until dawn. Many of the city's dance clubs are on the Richmond Street strip just south of Queen West, which is in itself home to a number of the live-music venues. The College Street area is also a good bet for searching out up-and-coming dance bars, though the area, with its many cafés and bistros, is more oriented toward a laid-back lounge crowd. When the clubs close (by 3am) the fearless night-owls seek out all-night raves that you can find out about only by word of mouth.

Polson Pier

An alternative to the downtown scene is the Polson Pier (▷ 72) entertainment complex, out on a limb in the Port of Toronto. It includes Toronto's largest lakeside patio, a concert-equipped nightclub, outdoor amusements and activities, even a drive-in movie theater.

City Hall; Gretzky's Bar on Windsor Street; Chinatown (top to bottom)

THEATRE DISTRICT

Since the mid-19th century, the area now known as the Theatre District has been animated with music halls, theaters and entertainment palaces. The opening of the Royal Alexandra Theatre in 1907 breathed life into the area. In 1989 the new SkyDome (now Rogers Centre) brought crowds of up to 55,000 into the district for baseball and other events. Restaurants and entertainment spots began springing up overnight, and the pace hasn't stopped.

Eating Out

Toronto is reputed to have no fewer than 7,000 restaurants, and though these include fast-food joints and neighborhood diners, you are still spoiled for choice with really excellent places to eat. This cosmopolitan city encompasses just about every major culture in its cuisine and prides itself on being Canada's trendsetter.

Neighborhood dining

The famous neighborhoods of Toronto make it easy to find a particular cuisine: Little Italy and Corso Italia; Greektown on the Danforth; Little India; Koreatown; Portugal Village; Little Poland; and a choice of Chinatowns. Shopping neighborhoods, such as Bloor/Yorkville, Yonge Street and the Fashion District, have plenty of eateries, and the entertainment district is full of places offering pre- and post-show dinners. You can even join the power-breakfast set in a Financial District eatery. If you happen upon a place where the locals go, you are guaranteed the best food and a great atmosphere.

Food Festivals

The best times to sample the various cuisines in Toronto is during one of the ethnic festivals: Chinese New Year (Jan/Feb); Taste of Little Italy (Jun); Caribana, Taste of the Danforth, Festival of South Asia and Muslimfest (Jul/Aug); and the Bloor West Village Ukrainian Festival and the Hispanic Fiesta (late Aug/early Sep). Canadian food is on offer at the Canadian National Exhibition (late Aug/early Sep), the Royal Agricultural Winter Fair (Nov) and the Canadian Aboriginal Festival (late Nov/early Dec).

TAKE TO THE LAKE

Try a brunch, lunch or dinner cruise on Lake Ontario. The views make this an appealing option. Prices are $45–$90, and some include dancing. Try: Mariposa Cruises (tel: 416/203-0178); Toronto Dinner Cruises (www.toronto-dinnercruises.com); Jubilee Queen (tel: 416/23-7245); or Great Lakes Schooner (tel: 416/203-2322).

Chinatown by day; freshly baked bread; Little Italy; alfresco dining in Little Italy (top to bottom)

Restaurants by Cuisine

With more than 7,000 restaurants and cafés, Toronto encompasses cuisines that are as multicultural as the city itself. For a more detailed description of each restaurant, see Toronto by Area.

AFRICAN

Sultan's Tent and Café Moroc (▷ 58)

CANADIAN/US

360 at the CN Tower (▷ 39, panel, 40)
Canoe (▷ panel, 40, 57)
Montana (▷ 40)
Senator (▷ 58)
Southern Accent (▷ 92)
Tundra (▷ 58)

CHINESE

Bright Pearl (▷ 39)
Wah Sing (▷ 40)

CONTINENTAL

Commodore's (▷ 74)
Future Bakery (▷ 92)
Rectory Café (▷ 74)
Richtree Market (▷ 57–58)
Scaramouche (▷ panel, 40)

DINER FARE

Fran's (▷ 57)
Island Paradise and Carousel Café (▷ 74)
Mr Greenjeans (▷ panel, 58)
Original Soup Man (▷ panel, 58)

ECLECTIC/FUSION

Boba (▷ 92)
Fred's Not Here (▷ 40)
Goldfish (▷ 92)
Matahari (▷ 40)
Olive and Lemon (▷ 92)
Senses (▷ 40)

FRENCH

Bb33 (▷ 57)
Bistro 990 (▷ 92)
Bloor Street Diner (▷ 92)
Bymark (▷ 57)
Gamelle (▷ 40)
Le Select (▷ 40)
Savoy Bistro (▷ 58)
Truffles (▷ 92)

ITALIAN

Alice Fazooli's (▷ 39)
Bar Italia (▷ 39)
Café Diplomatico (▷ 39)

JAPANESE

Ema-Tei (▷ 39–40)
Nami (▷ 57)

OTHER EUROPEAN

Chiado (▷ 39)
Esplanade Bier Markt (▷ 57)

PUB AND BAR FOOD

Crush (▷ 39)
Irish Embassy Pub and Grill (▷ 57)
Roof Lounge (▷ panel, 40)

SEAFOOD

Captain John's Harbour Boat (▷ 74)
Joso's (▷ 92)
Starfish (▷ 58)

STEAKS/GRILLS

Baton Rouge (▷ panel, 58)
Boat House Grill (▷ 74)
City Grill (▷ panel, 58)
Harbour Sixty Steak House (▷ 74)
Morton's of Chicago (▷ 92)
Ruth's Chris Steak House (▷ 58)

If You Like...

Sometimes, when a city has so much to offer, it's not so easy to focus on your particular interests and find out the best places to go. The following suggestions should help you tailor your ideal visit. Each sight or listing has a fuller write-up in Toronto by Area.

A MEAL WITH A VIEW

Splash out on a meal at 360 (▷ 39) and view the entire city as you revolve a full circle high up on the CN Tower.

Pick out a prime spot on a patio at a restaurants at the Boat House Grilll (▷ 74) at Queen's Quay Terminal (▷ 71) and watch all the activity on the lake.

Get room service at the Renaissance Toronto Downtown hotel (▷ 111) and watch a ball game from a room overlooking the Rogers Centre stadium (▷ 32).

Reserve a window seat at Canoe (▷ 57) and look down over the Financial District while savoring upscale Canadian cuisine.

Canoe restaurant (top); Rogers Centre (above)

CUTTING-EDGE CULTURE

Check out what's on at the Buddies in Bad Times Theatre (▷ 90), which stages productions that challenge social boundaries.

Explore unconventional works on display at the Museum of Contemporary Canadian Art (▷ 31).

Find out what came top in the annual awards at the Design Exchange (▷ 46–47).

Historic it may be, but the Distillery District (▷ 48–49) has a lively program of non-mainstream shows and events, from the Toronto Alternative Arts and Fashion Week to up-and-coming bands and innovative arts and crafts.

An art exhibition taking place in marquees in the Distillery District (above right); a blues concert attracts an appreciative audience in the Distillery District (right)

FRESH AIR AND EXERCISE

Rent a bicycle and pedal around the Toronto Islands (▷ 66–67).

Skim across Lake Ontario in a boat rented from the Queen's Quay Sailing and Power-boating Centre (▷ 63).

Take the subway to High Park (▷ 103) and hike through the natural forest of the Spring Creek and West Ravine nature trails.

Have a dip in the lake at The Beaches (▷ 103) or Toronto Islands (▷ 66–67).

Sign up, if you can, for the 'keeper for the day' program at Toronto Zoo (▷ 102); otherwise there's plenty of walking around the spacious enclosures.

INSIDE INFORMATION

Lectures by experts open up new insights at the Royal Ontario Museum (▷ 84–85)

The Ontario Science Centre (▷ 100–101) occasionally hosts presentations by members of the Royal Astronomical Society of Canada.

Head for St. Lawrence Market (▷ 51) any Saturday at noon for demonstrations by food experts, preceded by a short talk about the history of the market (in the South Market building).

Find out what the provincial government is up to by watching parliament in session at the Ontario Legislature (▷ 83).

A LAID-BACK AFTERNOON

Linger over a cappuccino and cake at Café Diplomatico (▷ 39) and absorb the atmosphere of Little Italy (▷ 33).

Escape the bustle of Yonge Street and savor the peaceful haven of the Allan Gardens (▷ 52).

Take a picnic to the Toronto Islands (▷ 66–67) and laze away the afternoon on the beach or under a shady tree.

Stretch out on the grass at the peaceful Musical Gardens (▷ 68), perhaps soothed by an open-air recital.

GREAT LIVE MUSIC

Check out Jeff Healey's Roadhouse
(▷ 37). All the performers are top class
even though the legendary guitarist himself is
no longer around.
More celebrity connections (Alex Lifeson of
Rush) guarantee top-notch rock, jazz, funk and
R&B at the Orbit Room (▷ 38).
Known for showcasing future stars from home
and abroad, the Horseshoe Tavern (▷ 37) is a
Toronto institution.
Chill out to the folk/acoustic performers in the
intimate C'Est What cellar bar (▷ 56).
Catch an open-air world music concert on
the Sirius Stage at the Harbourfront Centre
(▷ 72).
Join the crowds for a megastar concert at the
Molson Amphitheatre (▷ 65) or the Rogers
Centre (▷ 32).

WINDOW SHOPPING

Browse the dozen traders at Toronto Antiques
on King (▷ 36) for treasures that would never fit
in a suitcase.
Stroll around Bloor/Yorkville (▷ 89) with its
upscale boutiques—Prada, Chanel, Gucci, et al—and
see where the celebrities come to shop.
Wander along Queen Street West (▷ 35) for
cutting-edge Canadian fashion designers as well
as international couturiers.
Drool over the superstar designer footwear at
John Fluevog (▷ 36).

*Toronto has plenty of
outlets to hear blues
(top) and jazz (above)*

*Yorkville is Toronto's classy shopping
area, with plenty of designer names
(left and above)*

Toronto by Area

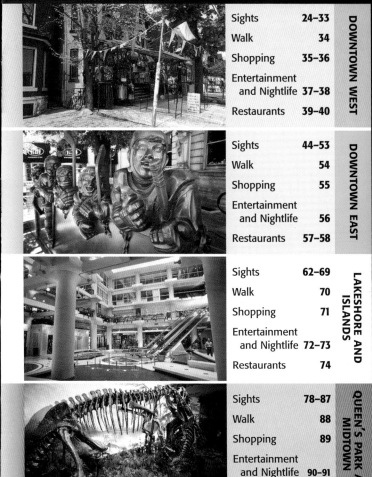

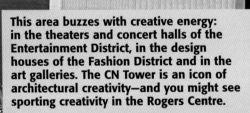

This area buzzes with creative energy:
in the theaters and concert halls of the
Entertainment District, in the design
houses of the Fashion District and in the
art galleries. The CN Tower is an icon of
architectural creativity—and you might see
sporting creativity in the Rogers Centre.

Art Gallery of Ontario

HIGHLIGHTS

- *Corpus* (Bernini)
- *The Massacre of the Innocents* (Rubens)
- *The Fire in the Saint-Jean Quartier, Seen Looking Westward* (Joseph Légaré)
- *West Wind* (Tom Thomson)

TIP

- The AGO restaurant is a cut above the usual museum café. It offers fine dining from a skilled chef, and organic ingredients sourced from sustainable farming.

The AGO, one of North America's finest art galleries, has been partially open during a massive expansion. In the fall of 2007 it closed completely to begin the reinstallation of art in the new galleries ready for a grand reopening in mid-2008.

New look The Transformation AGO project was sparked when Kenneth Thomson gifted his collection of some 2,000 works to the gallery, together with funding to help display them. More funds were raised to meet the $254 million cost. Toronto-born Frank Gehry's stunning design includes a soaring 200m (600ft) glass frontage along Dundas street, through which passersby can see into one of the sculpture galleries, a new four-story titanium-and-glass south wing, and major improvements to the existing building.

Clockwise from left: exterior of the gallery; children playing among some exhibits; a bronze sculpture at the entrance; provincial and national flags flying outside

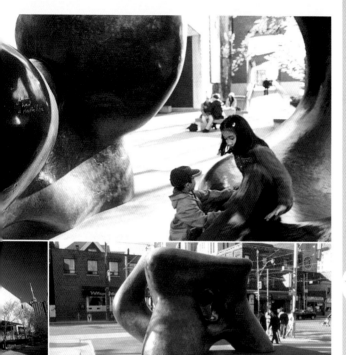

Collections The gallery has a total collection of around 66,000 works, covering many periods, genres and parts of the world. It also has a lively schedule of events, educational programs and community projects. The Canadian galleries are particularly interesting, ranging from First Nations art to the Group of Seven and innovative contemporary artists. There are also very important European works—the 17th-century collection is particularly good—along with works by Van Gogh, Picasso, Chagall, Modigliani, Gaugin, the surrealists and many others. The African and Australian aboriginal art collection is the finest in North America, and the AGO also houses the largest collection of Henry Moore works in the world, with plaster and bronze maquettes. You can hear recordings of Moore discussing his work and his affection for Toronto, and see some items that inspired him.

THE BASICS

www.ago.net

➕ K5

✉ 317 Dundas Street West

☎ 416/979-6648

🕐 Wed–Fri 10–9, Sat–Sun 10–5.30

🍽 Restaurant (tel 416/979-6612), café

Ⓟ St. Patrick

🚋 Dundas streetcar

♿ Very good

💰 Moderate

❓ Tours, lectures, films, concerts

The CN Tower

HIGHLIGHTS

- Glass floor
- SkyPod
- *Height of Excellence* movie
- Himalamazon motion theater rides
- The ride up

TIP

- Instead of rushing to the tower in the morning, wait until evening, head for the SkyPod and stay to watch the sun go down and the city lights go on. It's quite a sight.

The CN Tower, 553m (1,815ft) high, is Toronto's trademark. It was derided at first but ultimately embraced by citizens. Until the middle of 2007, the CN Tower was the tallest building in the world, then a hotel in Dubai overtook it on its way to a final height of 800m (2,624ft).

On a clear day It's certainly a stomach-churning experience to rocket up at 6m (20ft) per second in glass-fronted elevators to the Look Out level, where there are breathtaking views. Here you can stand—if you dare—on the Glass Floor, 342m (1,122ft) above the ground, then step out onto the outdoor observation deck, where, on a clear day, you can see the mist of Niagara Falls on the other side of the lake, though the safety netting detracts a little. Take the elevator another

Exterior and interior views of the tower, with the café on the observation deck and the view from the SkyPod windows

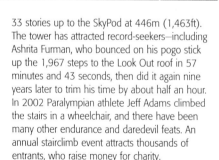

33 stories up to the SkyPod at 446m (1,463ft). The tower has attracted record-seekers—including Ashrita Furman, who bounced on his pogo stick up the 1,967 steps to the Look Out roof in 57 minutes and 43 seconds, then did it again nine years later to trim his time by about half an hour. In 2002 Paralympian athlete Jeff Adams climbed the stairs in a wheelchair, and there have been many other endurance and daredevil feats. An annual stairclimb event attracts thousands of entrants, who raise money for charity.

Shopping and other entertainments Down at the base of the tower there's hands-on action in the Arcade, featuring techno games and simulator rides. The Maple Leaf Theatre shows a 22-minute film on how the tower was built. The Marketplace offers varied shopping.

THE BASICS

www.cntower.ca

➕ K8

✉ 301 Front Street West

☎ 416/868-6937

🕐 Tower daily 8.30am–11pm (9am–10pm in winter). Other attractions vary

🍴 360 Restaurant, tel 416/362-5411, Horizons, Marketplace Café

🚇 Union Station

🚃 Front Street streetcar

♿ Very good

💰 Observation deck expensive; games expensive

Fort York

HIGHLIGHTS

- Officers' Quarters
- Stone Magazine
- Artillery demonstrations

This complex of buildings, sandwiched between the railroad tracks and the highway, will give you a historic jolt back to 1813 when muddy York was a rough-and-ready imperial outpost.

TIP

- Visit during July and August, when well-drilled, uniformed students perform guard drills, artillery demonstrations, military music and drumming.

Bicentenary preparations With the bicentenary of the War of 1812 (between the United States and Britain) approaching, improvements are underway at Fort York, including the reconstruction of a number of buildings within the complex. There are also new walkways and information points, with recorded stories available via cell phone. Many displays are also being brought up-to-date, so that visitors will more readily be engaged. A smart new Visitor Centre is also on the drawing board, but all the work is being undertaken with great sensitivity to the historic site.

Costumed interpreters and re-created rooms help visitors to imagine life in the fort during the 19th century

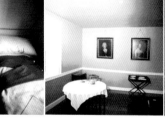

Fort York and the White House On April 27, 1813, during the War of 1812, 2,700 Americans stormed ashore from Lake Ontario. They drove out the troops at Fort York and set fire to Government House and the Parliament Buildings. In 1814, in retaliation, the British occupied Washington and burned the president's residence. According to Canadian legend, the Americans covered up the blackened walls with white paint, and from then it was called the White House, but the Americans say it was named for the color of the stone.

Military memorabilia John Graves Simcoe built a garrison on the site of Fort York in 1793. The fort was strengthened in 1811 (the west wall and circular battery date from that time) and, shortly after the events of 1813, the British rebuilt it; most of the fort's buildings date from then.

THE BASICS

www.toronto.ca/culture
www.forkyork.ca
🔂 G8
✉ Garrison Road, off Lakeshore Boulevard
☎ 416/392-6907
🕐 Victoria Day–Labour Day daily 10–5; rest of year Mon–Fri 10–4, Sat–Sun 10–5. May be closed for special events
🚋 Bathurst 511 streetcar
♿ Few
💷 Inexpensive
❓ Jul–end Aug: tours by interpreters in costume

Kensington Market

Colorful shops and goods for sale at Kensington Market

THE BASICS

www.kensington-market.ca

➕ H5

✉ Bounded by Spadina and Bellevue avenues and College and Dundas streets

🕐 Stores 11–7 (food stores open earlier)

🚋 Dundas or College streetcar

HIGHLIGHTS

- Mendel's Creamery
- Global Cheese
- Coral Seas Fish Market
- My Market Bakery
- Caribbean Corner
- Casa Acoreana
- Perola Supermarket

Colorful, quirky, a riot of street sounds and tempting aromas…and yet this is down-to-earth shopping among down-to-earth people. Kensington Market has grown out of a former Jewish enclave into a multiethnic hub where locals congregate and visitors come to enjoy the atmosphere. The federal government declared the market a National Historic Site in 2006.

Tastes of the World Culinary delights are the major draw here, but don't expect to find a central market square—there is just a series of narrow streets with stores selling a colorful array of food. Wander along Kensington and Augusta avenues and Baldwin Street for West Indian grocery stores full of sugar cane, plantains, yucca and the like, and for delicatessens, fresh fish stores and artisan cheeses from around the world. Augusta and Baldwin have health foods aplenty, too.

Street Vibe Food and history aside, there is an edgy, up-to-the minute feel about the place, with a lot of young fashion designers selling in the market boutiques (▷ The Rage, 36), and individualists combing the stores to create their own personal look, often with a "vintage" element. There's a café culture here, too, with intellectuals having earnest conversations, young people chilling out and visitors lingering over their coffee and drinking in the scene. Some of the cafés and restaurants have live music some evenings.

An exhibition at the museum (left); exterior view of the MOCCA building (right)

Museum of Contemporary Canadian Art

Founded in 1999 as the Art Gallery of North York, the Museum of Contemporary Canadian Art (MOCCA) moved to this new gallery in 2005, where it continues to make bold decisions and put together dynamic exhibitions.

Modern Canadian art The remit of the gallery is to present exciting and thought-provoking works that have been produced by Canadian artists over the past 20 years or so. It provides a splendid showcase to emerging as well as more established artists and offers some challenges for visiting art lovers. You could say it not so much breathes life into the Canadian art scene as applies a defibrillator and shouts "Clear!"

The collections The permanent collection amounts to around 400 works by around 150 artists including, not unexpectedly, some of the most influential new talent in Canada. These include the highly respected Stephen Andrews, Ivan Eyre, Arlene Stamp, Micah Lexier, Harold Klunder, Shelagh Keeley and many others. In addition to paintings and sculpture, there are works in other media, including video, installation, multimedia, photography and performance. Temporary exhibitions feature particular artists, a theme or an idea, sometimes totally Canadian, sometimes combined with the works of artists from other countries. The gallery also takes exhibitions from their own collection abroad to promote global awareness of Canadian art. The gallery is an exciting institution, run with vision and enthusiasm.

THE BASICS

www.mocca.toronto.on.ca

🔺 E6

✉ 952 Queen Street West at Shaw

☎ 416/395-7490

🕐 Tue–Sun 11–6

🚊 Queen Streetcar 501

♿ Good

🎟 Free

HIGHLIGHTS

● *Whitewatch* by Ivan Eyre
● *Book Sculptures: Brothers (Bunk Beds)* by Micah Lexier
● *Death Angel* by Harold Klunder

DOWNTOWN WEST

★

TOP 25

31

Rogers Centre

A full Rogers Centre with the roof retracted (left); a Blue Jays game (right)

THE BASICS

www.rogerscentre.com
🔲 K8
✉ 1 Blue Jays Way
☎ 416/341-1707, 416/341-2770 for tours; 416/341-1234 for tickets
🕐 Times vary, please call
🍴 Restaurants, cafés and snackbars
🚇 Union Station
🚋 Front Street streetcars
♿ Very good
🎟 Tours moderate

HIGHLIGHTS

● Retractable roof
● Video explaining the stadium's construction
● Corporate skyboxes
● Press facilities
● Dressing room
● Hotel overlooking the field

The home of the Blue Jays in downtown Toronto is so revolutionary in design that it has become an attraction with an organized tour. In the stadium hotel you can even rent a suite with a grandstand view of the field.

Engineering feat One of the largest Major League baseball stadiums ever built, Rogers has a fully retractable roof and required much engineering ingenuity in its design and execution. The 11,000-tonne roof covers nearly 3ha (8 acres) and there are 250,000 roof bolts, yet it can be opened in 20 minutes thanks to the ingenious steel track and the trucks driven by 10-horsepower motors. Although the tour film is cloying beyond belief, it does offer a glimpse of what it was like to build this vast structure. When the camera pans up the girders, their height is truly scary.

Tour topics On the tour, visitors are given a mass of statistics about the astroturf, and how long it takes for it all to be stuck together. You also visit one of the corporate skyboxes and take a look at the broadcast/press facilities. The stadium incorporates an 11-story hotel where the rooms have great views facing onto the field and can be rented on game nights for upward of $300. The Toronto Blue Jays Clubhouse is off limits to visitors, but you can have a peek (when events permit) at the visiting teams' dressing room. The Toronto Argonauts (Canadian Football League) also play here; other entertainment ranges from circuses to pop concerts and ice shows.

More to See

CBC BROADCAST CENTRE

www.cbc.ca/facilities

This distinctive work of architecture with a bright, colorful exterior, is one of the largest broadcasting centers in North America. In the grand Barbara Frum Atrium, named for the distinguished Canadian journalist and designed by Philip Johnson, you can see radio hosts speaking into microphones and technicians keeping everyone on track. The space is 10 floors high and topped with a skylight. The little museum (capacity 50 people) is fun and free. Enjoy a variety of clips from radio and TV, and the interactive exhibits. Special exhibitions have included radio sound effects and props from popular kids' programs, and the Graham Spry Theatre shows classic episodes of landmark TV shows.

✚ K7 ✉ 250 Front Street West
☎ 416/205-5574 ⏰ Mon–Fri 9–5
🍴 Cafeteria 🚇 Union ♿ Good

CHINATOWN

Sprawling along Dundas and Spadina, the original Chinatown bustles day and night as people shop at stands displaying brilliant green mustard and bok choy, fresh crabs and live fish, and herbal stores that sell "relaxing tea" and ginseng that costs hundreds of dollars for just one ounce. Today many of the businesses are operated by Thais and Vietnamese. It's a bright and colorful area, with street signs in Chinese as well as English, and restaurants are a big part of the attraction. Chinese New Year, with dragon dances and drumming, is a highlight.

✚ J5 🚇 St. Patrick 🚋 Dundas streetcar

LITTLE ITALY

http://littleitaly.sites.toronto.com

A vibrant Italian community thrives along College Street between Euclid and Shaw, where the street lamps bear neon maps of Italy. Old-style cafés with hissing espresso and cappuccino machines operate alongside more modern, fashionable establishments. At night, in particular, the area buzzes with energy as locals and visitors flock to the authentic restaurants.

✚ G3 🚋 College Street streetcar

The CBC Broadcast Centre

Chinatown at dusk

Downtown West Highlights

Start with the city's best view, then tour theaterland and a couple of colorful neighborhoods, with the superb AGO along the way.

DISTANCE: 3km (1.8 miles)   **ALLOW:** 2.5 hours

START

THE CN TOWER
⊞ K8 🚋 Front Street streetcar

END

KENSINGTON MARKET
⊞ H5 🚋 Dundas 505 streetcar

1 Walk east from The CN Tower along Front Street to check out the lobby-studios and museum of the CBC Broadcast Centre.

2 Backtrack, then turn right up John Street to King Street.

3 Turn right to see the Frank Stella murals in the Princess of Wales Theatre, then cross over to walk along the Canadian Walk of Fame, with Roy Thomson Hall to your right and the Royal Alexandra Theatre opposite.

4 Turn left and walk up Simcoe Street, bordering the Entertainment District, to Queen Street West.

8 Cross to the west side of Spadina and find Baldwin Street. Go down Baldwin Street into the heart of Kensington Market.

7 Exit the AGO on Dundas and go left through Chinatown, turning right on Spadina to explore more of this colorful neighborhood.

6 Turn right on John Street and walk north to enter Grange Park and the Art Gallery of Ontario.

5 Go left on Queen West to the Junction with John Street, stop at the corner to peek into Citytv's street-level studio to see who's on.

WALK

DOWNTOWN WEST

Shopping

ABRAHAM'S

This may not qualify as a high-end antiques store, but it is certainly a cherry-picker's delight. The space is jammed to the ceiling with all kinds of ephemera, from gas pumps to bicycles and neon beer signs to musical instruments.
H6 ✉ 635 Queen Street West ☎ 416/504-6210 🚋 Queen Street West streetcar

ALGONQUIANS SWEET GRASS GALLERY

Ojibway owned and run, the store has First Nations clothing and crafts, including carvings, jewelry and dreamcatchers.
G6 ✉ 668 Queen Street West ☎ 416/703-1336 🚋 Queen Street West streetcar

ANNE SPORTUN EXPERIMENTAL JEWELLERY

Designer Anne Sportun uses traditional gold-smithing techniques to make striking pieces inspired by nature and the universal language of shape and symbol. Richly colored precious stones are set in rings, earrings, necklaces or pendants. She will custom design as well.
F7 ✉ 742 Queen Street West ☎ 416/363-4114 🚋 Queen Street West streetcar

CABARET

The place to buy period costume and retro fashions. Seek out velvet and sequined gowns or that perfect smoking jacket.
G6 ✉ 672 Queen Street West (west of Palmerston) ☎ 416/504-7126 🚇 Osgoode 🚋 Queen Street West streetcar

CLUB MONACO

For casual, young fashions there is nowhere better than this chain, with several outlets in the city. This is the flagship store.
H6 ✉ 403 Queen Street West ☎ 416/979-5633 🚋 Queen Street West streetcar

DRAGON LADY COMIC SHOP

Try here if you are looking

QUEEN STREET WEST

This is the hip shopping area where Canada's young designers rule, and foreign designers, such as Vivienne Westwood and Valentino, are also well represented. You will certainly be spoiled for choice with all the fashion boutiques, vintage clothing stores, flamboyant shoes, jewelry and homewares. The trendy bars and cafés are good for people-watching and celebrity-spotting too. Try the Queen Mother Café at No. 208, just west of University Avenue, or Niche, farther along at No. 626.

---

for an unusual, reasonably priced gift. It sells comics dating back to 1950, posters and back issues of *Life* magazine.
G4 ✉ 609 College Street at University ☎ 416/536-7460 🚋 College

FREDA'S

Canadian designer Freda Iordanous dresses TV personalities and actresses, and all her casual, business and evening garments for women (in sizes 4 to 20) are produced on the premises. Lines from Europe are also stocked.
G7 ✉ 86 Bathurst Street ☎ 416/703-0304 or 1-888/373-3271 🚋 Bathurst or King Street West

F/X

Outrageous fashions, including those by (eccentric) British trendsetter Vivienne Westwood, fill the racks at this hip store.
H6 ✉ 515 Queen Street West ☎ 416/504-0888 🚋 Queen Street West streetcar

GOTSTYLE

A cool place in the Fashion District for modern menswear, with designer brands, independent labels, accessories, shoes. There are leather sofas, sport on TV and a men-only spa.
H7 ✉ 489 King Street West ☎ 416/260-9696 🚋 King Street West or Spadina streetcar

JOHN FLUEVOG

The most flamboyant shoes you can imagine are found at this ultrahip outlet. Madonna and Paula Abdul have been known to shop here.
K6 242 Queen Street West 416/581-1420 Osgoode Queen Street West streetcar

LEGENDS OF THE GAME

Sports fans head here to purchase the shirt, hat or signed gear of their favorite team or player.
K7 322A King Street West 416/971-8848 St. Andrew

MOUNTAIN EQUIP-MENT CO-OP

Even if you're not a climber, you'll find great outdoor clothing, footwear and camping gear here. The store's roof is a sustainable re-creation of a prairie environment and the store takes in used (clean) polyester clothing for recycling.
J7 400 King Street West 416/340-2667 King Street West or Spadina streetcar

PRIME GALLERY

Inspiring and appealing ceramic and other crafted objects, terra-cotta, fabric and jewelry—ranging in price from reasonable to very expensive.
K6 52 McCaul Street 416/593-5750 Osgoode

THE RAGE

Toronto's innovative fashion students have an outlet here for their cutting-edge, unique and affordable designs. It's a great place for hip individualists to create their own look. Stock changes all the time.
J5 13 Kensington Avenue 416/588-5177 Dundas Street West or Spadina streetcar

RHYTHM CORNER

Independent music store specializing in reggae, calypso and gospel on CD and vinyl.
J5 60 Kensington Avenue 416/260-8412

BOOKSTORES GALORE

Toronto's bookstore scene remains healthy in spite of the recent closure of a few loved small stores. The national chain Indigo/Chapters have lots of outlets, including the former Coles chain and the World's Biggest Bookstore, which have both been swallowed up. Local independents include the elegant **Nicholas Hoare Ltd** (▷ 55), which offers less mainstream choices, **Pages Books and Magazines** (K6 256 Queen Street West 416/598-1447) and **Book City**, with five stores: Yonge Street, Danforth Avenue, Queen Street East, and two on Bloor Street West.

Dundas Street West or Spadina streetcar

STEVEN TEMPLE BOOKS

Founded in 1974, this is one of oldest bookstores in the city, with an excellent selection of Canadian literature. Don't expect to find any paperbacks or magazines here.
H6 489 Queen Street West, 2nd Floor 416/703-9980 Queen Street West streetcar

TEN REN TEA

In the heart of Chinatown, this store stocks fine teas in urns and also sells health-oriented infusions and slimming tea. You will also find stocks of tiny, Chinese teapots and teacups.
J5 454 Dundas Street West at Huron 416/598-7872 Dundas streetcar

TORONTO ANTIQUES ON KING

High-quality dealers, who are well known in their specialties, operate the dozen booths here. Shoppers will find estate jewelry, maps and prints, porcelain, silver, Oriental rugs, scientific instruments and more.
K7 267 King Street West at Duncan 416/345-9941 St. Andrew

Entertainment and Nightlife

BAR ITALIA
www.bar-italia.ca
The slick spot in Little Italy for the young and beautiful. Upstairs there's a plush lounge area. Downstairs it's coffee, alcohol and Italian specialties all round.
�'t G4 ✉ 582 College Street ☎ 416/535-3621 🚋 College Street streetcar

EL CONVENTO RICO
www.elconventorico.com
Famed for its weekend 1am drag shows. Lambada the night away until 4am.
🔗 F3 ✉ 750 College Street at Crawford ☎ 416/588-7800 🚋 College streetcar west

CROCODILE ROCK
www.crocrock.ca
Bar-restaurant and dance space with pool lounge. The crowd grooves to 70s and 80s dance sounds.
🔗 K6 ✉ 240 Adelaide Street West at Duncan ☎ 416/599-9751 🚇 St. Andrew

DRAKE HOTEL BAR
In an artsy hotel there's an eclectic program of live music and DJs. Offerings include soul, funk, reggae, jazz, opera and French *chanson*.
🔗 D6 ✉ 1150 Queen Street West ☎ 416/531-5042 🚋 Queen Street West streetcar

EASY & THE FIFTH
An older crowd (and sometimes visiting celebrities) gathers in the loft-like space. The music leans to lounge and even allows for conversation.
🔗 K6 ✉ 225 Richmond Street West ☎ 416/979-3000 🚇 Osgoode

FACTORY THEATRE
www.factorytheatre.ca
Dedicated to producing the works of new Canadian playwrights, which are put on in two theaters. Many of the company's productions have been on international tours and have had some success abroad.
🔗 H6 ✉ 125 Bathurst ☎ 416/504-9971 🚋 Bathurst streetcar

FAMOUS PEOPLE PLAYERS DINNER THEATRE
www.fpp.org
This group specializes in the unique black light theater. Black-clad players move around manipulating lifesize puppets of famous people and props. The bar was sponsored by the actor Paul Newman and the theater is named for Phil Collins, who has been a great inspiration.
🔗 D6 ✉ 110 Sudbury Street ☎ 416/532-1137 🚋 Queen streetcar to Dovercourt

FLUID LOUNGE
www.fluidlounge.ca
Good-looking and hip dressers gain entry to the "underwater-styled" venue to dance to the neo funk, industrial and other up-to-the-minute music. Check for celebs.
🔗 K6 ✉ 217 Richmond Street West ☎ 416/593-6116 🚇 Osgoode

HORSESHOE TAVERN
www.horseshoetavern.com
Sixty years old in 2007, this is the place where The Police, The Band, Blue Rodeo and Barenaked Ladies got their start in Canada.
🔗 J6 ✉ 370 Queen Street West ☎ 416/598-4753 🚋 Queen Street West streetcar

JEFF HEALEY'S ROADHOUSE
www.jeffhealey.com
The finest rock, blues and jazz acts continue to be presented at the late Toronto guitar legend Jeff Healey's club. There are also jams and comedy open-mic nights.
🔗 J7 ✉ 56 Blue Jays Way ☎ 416/593-2626 🚇 Union Station 🚋 Spadina streetcar

TICKETS & INFORMATION
Get tickets, including day-of-performance half-price admission, at the TO Tix booth at Yonge-Dundas Square (🔗 M5 🚇 Tue–Sat 12–6.30 ☎ 1-888/222-6608). To find out what's on, try *Toronto Life*, *Where Toronto* and the weekend editions of the *Globe & Mail*, *Toronto Star* and *Toronto Sun*. *Eye* or *Now* cover the hip scene, *Xtra!* gay action.

ORBIT ROOM

www.orbitroom.ca

Co-founded by Alex Lifeson of Rush, this continues to be a premier venue for live R&B, funk, alternative rock and jazz.
➕ G4 ✉ 580A College Street ☎ 416/535-0613 🚃 College streetcar

PRINCESS OF WALES THEATRE

www.mirvish.com

Opened in 1993, this 2,000-seat theater has one of the largest stages in North America and three-level seating giving excellent sight-lines. The acoustics are near perfect. Craftsmanship is superb and the murals alone are worth a visit. The North American premiere of Andrew Lloyd Webber's production of *The Sound of Music* is scheduled for the fall of 2008.
➕ K7 ✉ King Street West at John Street ☎ 416/872-1212, 1-800/461-3333 tickets, 416/593-0351 admin

REX HOTEL JAZZ AND BLUES BAR

www.therex.ca

This club offers top local and up-and-coming modern jazz artists.
➕ K6 ✉ 194 Queen Street West ☎ 416/598-2475 🚃 Queen Street West streetcar

RIVOLI

www.rivoli.ca

Hip club-restaurant for an eclectic mix of grunge, blues, rock, jazz, indie and comedy.
➕ J6 ✉ 334 Queen Street West ☎ 416/596-1908 🚇 Osgoode 🚃 Queen Street West streetcar

ROYAL ALEXANDRA THEATRE

www.mirvish.com

The century-old theater has been played by many of the all-time greats of the stage, including John Gielgud, Orson Welles, Fred Astaire, and the Marx Brothers. The interior remains the epitome of a 19th-century theater.
➕ K7 ✉ King Street West at Duncan ☎ 416/872-1212, 1-800/461-3333 tickets, 416/593-0351 admin

ROY THOMSON HALL

www.roythomson.com

This is the foremost concert hall in Canada. The greatest international orchestras and classical performers play here,

CLASSICAL COMPANIES

Two Toronto institutions perform principally at Roy Thomson Hall. The Toronto Symphony is the city's premier orchestra. In addition to its classical repertoire, it plays light popular music and its outdoor summer concerts are well supported. The Toronto Mendelssohn Choir performs great choral works, and is noted for Handel's *Messiah*. The choir performed on the soundtrack of the movie *Schindler's List*.

with occasional world culture and other genres.
➕ K7 ✉ 60 Simcoe Street ☎ 416/872-4255 box office, 416/593-4822 admin

SECOND CITY

www.secondcity.com

This venue is the source of many Canadian comedians who have made it big internationally—Mike Myers, John Candy, Dan Aykroyd, Bill Murray, Martin Short, and others.
➕ J7 ✉ 51 Mercer Street ☎ 416/343-0011 🚇 Union

THEATRE PASSE MURAILLE

www.passemuraille.co.ca

This is another company that nurtures contemporary Canadian playwrights. It produces innovative and provocative works by such figures as Daniel David Moses and Wajdi Mouawad. There are two stages, one catering for an audience of 160, the other for just 64.
➕ H6 ✉ 16 Ryerson Avenue ☎ 416/504-7529 🚃 Queen Street West streetcar or streetcar south from Bathurst

TONIC

www.tonicnightclub.com

A specialized theatrical environment with freedom and movement in a fresh, modern context. The world's first ever multimedia light show; 72 TVs hover over a central dance space.
➕ H8 ✉ 117 Peter Street ☎ 416/204-9200 🚃 Queen streetcar to Peter

Restaurants

DOWNTOWN WEST

RESTAURANTS

PRICES

Prices are approximate, based on a 3-course meal for one person.

$$$$	over $80
$$$	$60–$80
$$	$35–$60
$	under $35

360 AT THE CN TOWER ($$$$)

www.cntower.ca

Don't write this revolving restaurant off as a tourist trap. It is, in fact, a fine-dining experience, with an extensive à la carte menu of impressive dishes that make the best use of Canadian produce, including prime beef, Atlantic salmon and lobster, and Ontario pickerel. Superb wine list.

➕ K8 ✉ 301 Front Street West ☎ 416/362-5411
🕐 Lunch and dinner daily
Ⓜ Union

ALICE FAZOOLI'S ($$)

www.alicefazoolis.com

In the Entertainment District, this is a lovely renovated old warehouse with a separate cocktail bar. The food is classic Italian, from lunchtime paninis to antipasti, seafood fettuccine or veal parmigiana.

➕ K6 ✉ 294 Adelaide Street West ☎ 416/979-1910
🕐 Lunch and dinner daily
Ⓜ Osgoode or St. Andrew

BAR ITALIA ($$)

www.bar-italia.ca

Italian chic with an upstairs pool hall and a downstairs café jammed at night with a young crowd.

➕ F4 ✉ 582 College Street
☎ 416/535-3621
🕐 Mon–Thu 11am–midnight, Fri 11am–2am, Sat 10am–2am, Sun 10am–1am ☒ College Street streetcar

BRIGHT PEARL ($)

www.brightpearlseafood.com

Don't visit Chinatown without stopping in for a meal at this renowned Chinese seafood restaurant—you can't miss its bright yellow-and-green facade. Dim Sum is on the go all day long, with 80 to 100 choices on the carts, and the 2-course Peking duck alone is worth a special journey.

➕ J5 ✉ 346–348 Spadina Avenue ☎ 416/979-3988
🕐 Daily 9am–11pm
☒ Spadina or Dundas Street West streetcar

A FEW TIPS

Restaurant checks (bills) include a 5 percent goods and service tax (GST), and 8 percent provincial sales tax (PST), which together equal 15 percent tax. Always tip on the pretax total of the check. Most restaurants are smoke-free. Call first if this is important to you. Well-dressed casual is acceptable in most restaurants. Men might feel more comfortable wearing a jacket in the more upscale dining spots.

CAFÉ DIPLOMATICO ($)

www.diplomatico.ca

Still not gussied up, it has mosaic marble floors, wrought-iron chairs and a glorious cappuccino machine. A Toronto tradition on weekends.

➕ G4 ✉ 594 College Street
☎ 416/534-4637
🕐 Sun–Thu 8am–1am, Fri, Sat 8am–3am ☒ College Street streetcar

CHIADO ($$$)

www.chiadorestaurant.ca

Reminiscent of a Lisbon bistro. Stick to such signature Portuguese dishes as the marinated sardines, poached salted cod and the nato do céu.

➕ E3 ✉ 864 College Street, at Concord Avenue
☎ 416/538-1910 🕐 Lunch Mon–Fri, dinner daily
☒ College Street streetcar

CRUSH ($$)

www.crushwinebar.com

Not just a wine bar, the food is good, too. The open kitchen in this handsome warehouse space serves contemporary mains and small plates. You'll find game as well as vegetarian dishes. The $58 prix fixe is good.

➕ J7 ✉ 455 King Street West at Spadina ☎ 416/977-1234 🕐 Lunch Mon–Fri, dinner Mon–Sat ☒ King/St. Andrew

EMA-TEI ($$)

Frequented by many Japanese visitors to Toronto because it

delivers absolutely authentic cuisine, from the perfect appetizers to the fresh sushi.

➕ K6 ✉ 30 St. Patrick Street ☎ 416/340-0472 🕐 Lunch Mon–Fri, dinner daily 🚇 Osgoode

FRED'S NOT HERE ($$)
www.fredsnothere.com
A huge, glowing mural and an open kitchen share the limelight with a long, eclectic menu of interesting dishes. Mediterranean and Oriental influences are in evidence alongside comfort food such as slow-roasted venison or a pork and sausage combo with celeriac mash.

➕ K6 ✉ 321 King Street West ☎ 416/971-9155 🕐 Mon–Fri 11.30–2.30, 5–10 (to 11pm Thu–Sat) 🚋 King Street West streetcar

GAMELLE ($$)
www.gamelle.com
A gem of a bistro. The proprietor-chef uses super-fresh ingredients in carefully prepared dishes, often inspired by Provence. Warm personal service, too.

➕ G4 ✉ 468 College Street at Markham ☎ 416/923-6254 🕐 Lunch Tue–Fri, dinner Mon–Sat 🚋 College or Bathurst streetcar

MATAHARI ($)
www.mataharigrill.com
Coconut-scented curries, really fresh fish enhanced by sauces spiced with

lime leaf, chilis and red onion, spring rolls and satays, all served in a halogen-lit setting.

➕ J4 ✉ 39 Baldwin Street (off Spadina) ☎ 416/596-2832 🕐 Lunch Tue–Fri, dinner Tue–Sun 🚇 St. Patrick

MONTANA ($$)
A lively spot in the Entertainment District with stylish decor, friendly staff and a sports bar and music venue upstairs. The menu offers classic Canadian favorites, including chicken and ribs combo, steaks, pizza and really good burgers. Great cocktails too.

➕ K6 ✉ 145 John Street ☎ 416/595-5949 🕐 Daily from 11.30am 🚇 Osgoode 🚋 Queen Street West streetcar

LE SELECT ($–$$)
www.leselect.com
In its new location, Le

TABLES WITH A VIEW

On the 54th floor of Mies van der Rohe's TDC, **Canoe** offers a view of surrounding skyscrapers. At the top of the Park Hyatt, the **Roof Lounge** (✉ 4 Avenue Road ☎ 416/925-1234) affords great views of downtown. **Scaramouche** (✉ 1 Benvenuto Place ☎ 416/961-8011) has window seats on the downtown skyline. The most stunning view of all is from **360** on top of the CN Tower (▷ 39).

Select is still as French as they come, from the *pied-de-cochon* to the background jazz.

➕ H7 ✉ 432 Wellington Street West ☎ 416/596-6405 🕐 Mon–Wed 11.30–11, Thu–Fri 11.30–11.30, Sat 11am–midnight, Sun 10.30–10.30 🚋 King Street West streetcar

SENSES ($$$)
www.metropolitan.com/soho/restaurants
Sophisticated, clean lines are the hallmark of this 40-seat restaurant in one of the city's newest luxury hotels. Signature dishes favor triple searing of meats. Pristine cooking gives us fish poached in seaweed broth. Desserts to die for.

➕ J7 ✉ Soho Metropolitan Hotel, 328 Wellington Street West ☎ 416/935-0400 🕐 Dinner only Tue–Sat 🚇 Union 🚋 King streetcar

WAH SING ($)
A mealtime mecca, where the seafood tank is often filled with giant, queen crabs ready to sizzle with ginger and onion. Also worth looking out for are the deep-fried oysters, duck with Peking sauce and, in season, two lobsters for the price of one.

➕ K4 ✉ 47 Baldwin Street ☎ 416/599-8822 🕐 Daily 11.30–11 🚋 Dundas West streetcar

This is the financial, commercial and administrative heart of the city. But there's entertainment, historic sights, and hockey heroes at the Air Canada Centre and Hockey Hall of Fame. Much of the PATH underground city is beneath these streets.

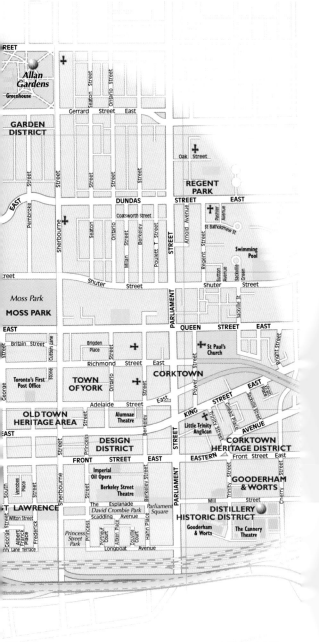

Lake Ontario

HIGHLIGHTS

- Council Chamber
- Hall of Memory
- Nathan Phillips Square
- *Metropolis*
- Henry Moore's *Three Way Piece Number Two* ("The Archer")
- Peace Garden
- Reflecting pool

TIP

- Guided tours are only available to groups, but the website has a good down-loadable self-guiding tour.

Remarkable for its striking design, which shook up Toronto in the early 1960s, City Hall could be a space station, with the council chamber a flying saucer cradled between two semicircular control towers.

Viljo Revell and Nathan Phillips When Mayor Nathan Phillips persuaded the City Council to hold a competition to design a new city hall, the councillors received 520 submissions from 42 countries. Finnish architect Viljo Revell was announced the winner, and his building opened in 1965. The square in front serves as a site for entertainment; the reflecting pool, where workers eat sandwiches in summer, turns into a skating rink in winter. To the east of City Hall, the Peace Garden contains an eternal flame lit by Pope John Paul II using a flame from the Memorial for Peace

Clockwise from left: City Hall with the old town hall clock tower; nighttime view from above; the Peace Garden; Henry Moore's sculpture The Archer; daytime view of City Hall from below

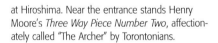

at Hiroshima. Near the entrance stands Henry Moore's *Three Way Piece Number Two*, affectionately called "The Archer" by Torontonians.

Municipal art City Hall itself contains several art works. Just inside the entrance, the mural *Metropolis*, by local artist David Partridge, is created from more than 100,000 nails. Continue into the Rotunda and the Hall of Memory, shaped like a sunken amphitheater, where, in the Golden Book of Remembrance, are listed 3,500 Torontonians who died in World War II. At its center rises a large white column supporting the Council Chamber above. The north corridor is lined with a copper-and-glass mosaic called *Views to the City*, depicting historic panoramic views of the city skyline. From here you can take an elevator up to the Council Chamber.

THE BASICS

www.toronto.ca

➕ L6

✉ 100 Queen Street West

☎ 416/338-0338

🕐 Mon–Fri 8.30–4.30

🍴 Cafeteria

🚇 Queen or Osgoode

♿ Very good

💲 Free

❓ Self-guided tour

Design Exchange

Housed in the former Stock Exchange—a splendid Moderne building with its architectural features preserved—the Design Exchange was established in the 1980s to promote Canadian design and to encourage more appreciation of applied arts.

The building In 1986 the city council was persuaded that a design center would be a good idea, but it wasn't until 1994 that it held its official opening in the fine heritage building recently vacated by the Toronto Stock Exchange. Now encased by the TD Centre, the pink granite and limestone facade stands out against the surrounding black-and-glass structure—a frame that serves to emphasize the symmetry of the early 20th-century design. Inside is equally impressive, with some remarkable murals and a fine staircase.

Clockwise from left: the exterior of the building; northeast view of the trading floor of the old Stock Exchange; staircase of the trading floor; murals

The exhibits No other museum in Canada has a collection that is so focused on the preservation of the nation's modern industrial design. The permanent collection includes more than 150 items of furniture, graphic design, industrial design, homewares, decorative arts, sporting goods and other themes. It's fun to look back over the past 70 years of chair design and to see the first item acquired by the Design Exchange—the stylish but bulky Project G2 Stereo. The DX stages exhibitions every year to highlight aspects of design, in the Chalmers Design Centre and Teknion Lounge at ground level and in the 3rd-floor Exhibition Hall. Recent exhibitions have included themes on ecological and sustainable architecture, book design, "Canada in the Making" and traveling exhibitions from Japan, Denmark and Italy. A highlight of the year is the Design Exchange Awards.

THE BASICS

www.dx.org

➕ L7

✉ 234 Bay Street

☎ 416/363-6121

🕐 Mon–Fri 9–5, Sat–Sun 12–5

🍽 Restaurants, café and food hall in TD Centre

🚇 King or Union Station

🚃 King Street 504 streetcar

♿ Very good

💲 Inexpensive

❓ Tours Mon–Fri 2pm

Distillery Historic District

HIGHLIGHTS

● Wandering the cobbled streets between historic buildings
● Distillery Walking Tour and Segway tours
● Glass artists at work in the Tank studio
● Sandra Ainsley Glass Gallery
● Jane Corkin photographic gallery
● Mill Street Brewery tour

TIP

● Movie, TV and music video filming might occasionally block off some areas. On the plus side, you might spot some famous actors and singers.

Vibrant, artsy and atmospheric, a place to shop for artisan crafts and original art, a venue for live music and festivals: It is indeed a far cry from the rundown, deserted former distillery that until recently covered this out-of-the-way site.

Where it began William Gooderham's and James Worts' waterfront distillery started up in 1837, and in just 10 years it had become the world's largest distillery. In 1987, this outstanding example of Victorian industrial design was acquired by Allied Lyons, who spent $25 million on its preservation.

Everything old is new In December 2001, local visionary developers purchased the 13-acre (5ha) site and set about installing new life. Original concrete floors, brick walls and beamed ceilings

Clockwise from left: Balzacs Coffee Roastery; Trinity Street at night; an aerial view of Trinity Street; Tank House Lane

remain unchanged. More than 340,000 old bricks from Cleveland have been laid in the lanes and alleyways, and a contemporary, creative group of tenants now inhabit the atmospheric buildings.

Arts and culture A jazz festival marked the opening in May 2003 and about 30 festivals still take place each year. Original distillery buildings now house a microbrewery making Ontario's first organic beer, art galleries, nearly 20 artists' studios and lots of interesting stores and boutiques. Goods range from clothing and jewelry to furniture. The performing arts have a large presence, including theater and dance companies and performance schools. The Young Centre for the Performing Arts, with partners George Brown College and Soulpepper Theatre, occupy a complex that includes four performing spaces.

THE BASICS

www.thedistillerydistrict. com

🗺 Q7

✉ Between Mill Street, Parliament Street and Cherry Street

☎ 416/364-1177; tours 1-866/405-8687

🕐 Site opens 10am; stores and galleries, hours vary

🍴 Many outlets

🚇 Union Station, then 65 or 65A Parliament bus

🚋 King 504 streetcar to Parliament Street, then walk south

♿ Good

💲 Free; tours moderate

❓ Various tours

Hockey Hall of Fame

Exhibits (left); replica of the Stanley Cup (right)

THE BASICS

www.hhof.com

M7

Brookfield Place at
30 Yonge Street

416/360-7765

Late Jun–early Sep and
Mar break Mon–Sat 9.30–6,
Sun 10–6; Sep–end May
Mon–Fri 10–5, Sat 9.30–6,
Sun 10.30–5

King or Union Station

King Street streetcar

Very good

Expensive

HIGHLIGHTS

● Stanley Cup
● Rink Zone
● Montréal Canadiens'
dressing room
● Impact Zone
● The Stanley Cup Odyssey

There's a Canadian saying: First you walk, then you skate. Hockey is to Canadians what football is to the Americans. It's the one game that most Canadians want to watch and take part in.

The Stanley Cup and Hall of Fame The jewel of the museum is the Bell Great Hall, once the grand banking hall of the Bank of Montreal. Here the Stanley Cup, North America's oldest professional sports trophy, is displayed in front of the Honoured Members Wall.

Live action At the Be a Player Zone you will find live shooting booths with sticks and a pail full of pucks; or you can test your skills against goalkeeper Ed Balfour, on a life-size computer simulation; or you can pad up and play against Wayne Gretzky and Mark Messier, who fire sponge pucks at full speed from a video screen.

A hockey tour From the entrance lobby, you pass into the NHL Zone, with multimedia displays and memorabilia about all aspects of the NHL and its milestone moments and teams. From there it's an exciting journey through the world of hockey, including an interactive Broadcast Zone, simulators, theaters showing hockey events, displays of artifacts and trophies, a re-creation of the Montréal Canadiens locker room, places to pick up some memorabilia of your own, and more. Before you leave check out the fun *Our Game* bronze and *Team Canada '72* monument outside the building.

The lofty 19th-century building that houses this market is entirely worthy of the rich and colorful displays within. This is the place to taste a Canadian peameal bacon sandwich or amass the ingredients for a picnic banquet.

Food-lovers' favorites There are more than 50 vendors in the market, all of them experts in their own specialty, and the array of cheeses, meats, vegetables, deli goods, seafood, baked goods and gourmet treats is irresistible. At Sausage King you'll find 10 or more types of salami. Combine any one with the breads at the Carousel Bakery or grab a peameal bacon sandwich for breakfast (the flavor of the bacon is deliciously enriched by its coating of ground dried peas). Go to Mano's Meats for pastrami or corned beef on a bun with plenty of kraut, relish and mustard. Great wheels of cheese can be found at Alex Farm Products, from Stilton to Camembert. Any picnic will be enhanced by the chocolate butter tarts, skor brownies or other pastries sold at Future Bakery. And for good measure, why not throw in some Quebec terrines (rabbit and pistachio, wild boar and apricot, pheasant and mushroom), pâtés, or shrimp and lobster mousse from Scheffler's Deli? Downstairs there's more, including Caviar Direct and 33 different kinds of rice at Rube's.

Fresh from the fields On Saturday farmers set up stalls at daybreak in the Farmers' Market building across the street, selling fresh produce, preserves, fresh baking, meat, and arts and crafts.

THE BASICS

www.stlawrencemarket.com
- N7
- 92 Front Street East
- 416/392-7219
- Tue–Thu 8–6, Fri 8–7, Sat 5–5; farmers' market Sat from 5am
- King or Union
- King Street streetcars
- Good
- Free

HIGHLIGHTS

- Sausage King
- Carousel Bakery
- Mano's Meats
- Future Bakery
- Scheffler's Deli
- Alex Farm Products
- Caviar Direct

More to See

ALLAN GARDENS

Just a short way east of busy Yonge Street, this peaceful haven is a horticultural gem. It has six greenhouses, of which the best is the glass-domed Palm House, modeled on the one at Kew Gardens in London, which stands here in radiant Victorian glory.

➕ N4 ✉ 19 Horticultural Avenue, off Gerrard Street ☎ 416/392-7288 🕐 Daily 10–5 🚇 College ♿ Good 🎟 Free

EATON CENTRE

www.torontoeatoncentre.com

Timothy Eaton emigrated from Ireland in 1854 and set up shop in St. Mary's, Ontario. He arrived in Toronto in 1869 and opened a store on Yonge Street, where he started innovative merchandizing and marketing, like fixed prices, cash-only sales, refunds and mail order—all unique then. Sadly, Eaton's was eventually swallowed up in the Sears Canada group (▷ 55). Enter at the southern end to see the splendor of Ed Zeidler's 264m (866ft) galleria and the sculptured flock of 60 Canada geese in flight by Michael Snow.

➕ M5 ✉ Dundas and Yonge to Queen and Yonge ☎ 416/598-8760 🕐 Mon–Fri 10–9, Sat 9.30–7, Sun 12–6 🍴 Several restaurants plus food court 🚇 Dundas or Queen ♿ Very good 🎟 Free

MACKENZIE HOUSE

Toronto's first mayor, William Lyon Mackenzie, lived in this house from 1859 until his death in 1861 and it now acts as a museum recalling the life of this feisty, fiery Scotsman. As an outspoken journalist, he published the *Colonial Advocate*, and the house has a re-creation of his printshop. Other displays recall his turbulent political life, including the unsuccessful Upper Canada Rebellion that he led.

➕ M5 ✉ 82 Bond Street ☎ 416/392-6915 🕐 May–early Sep Tue–Sun 12–5; Sep–Dec Tue–Fri 12–4, Sat–Sun 12–5; Jan–Apr Sat–Sun 12–5 🚇 Dundas ♿ Few 🎟 Inexpensive

OSGOODE HALL

www.osgoodehall.com

This building (1829) houses the headquarters of Ontario's legal

The colorful Allan Gardens

Eaton Centre and the sculptured geese by Michael Snow

profession, with an elegant interior and an impressive portrait and sculpture collection. There are many rooms to see, including the stunning Great Library and American Room, the courtrooms, and Convocation Hall, with its superb stained-glass windows. Throughout, there are outstanding tiled floors and other architectural features. The building is set in grounds of lawns and flower beds.

➕ L6 ✉ 130 Queen Street West
☎ 416/947-3300 or 416/327-5079
🕐 Mon–Fri 8.30–5 🚇 Osgoode ♿ Few
🎫 Free

TEXTILE MUSEUM OF CANADA
www.textilemuseum.ca
This gem of a museum has a huge permanent collection of 12,000 textiles, some as old as 2,000 years, from all over the world. There are also changing exhibitions offering collections that are esthetically engaging as well as of anthropological interest.

➕ L5 ✉ 55 Centre Avenue
☎ 416/599-5321 🕐 Daily 11–5 (Wed to 8)
🚇 St. Patrick ♿ Very good 🎫 Moderate

TORONTO SCULPTURE GARDEN
www.torontosculpturegarden.com
A serene retreat established in 1981 in a city park. Two installations annually feature works by Canadian and international artists. The space offers artists the chance to experiment in a public context. The works are for sale.

➕ N7 ✉ 115 King Street East at Church
☎ 416/515-9658 🕐 Daily 8–dusk 🚇 King
🎫 Free

TRINITY SQUARE AND TORONTO PUBLIC LABYRINTH
When plans for the Eaton Centre were drawn up, they called for the demolition of the Church of the Holy Trinity. Fortunately it was saved, and now sits in a little park just west of the Eaton Centre. Built in 1847, the church now overlooks a labyrinth, some 23m (77ft) across, which was installed in 2005. The theory is that by walking in these ever-decreasing circles you will center yourself and thus aid creative thinking or gain a problem-solving mind-set. It's worth a try.

➕ M5 🚇 Dundas

A splendid hat on display (above) and a silk kimono (right) at the Textile Museum of Canada

Historic Highlights

Explore some of Toronto's oldest areas, including the Distillery Historic District and one of the best food markets in Canada.

DISTANCE: 3km (2 miles) **ALLOW:** 3 hours

START

UNION STATION
🚇 L7 Ⓜ Union Square

END

TORONTO SCULPTURE PARK
🚇 N7 Ⓜ King

1 From Union Station, walk east on Front Street, cross over Yonge Street to pass the Hummingbird Centre and St. Lawrence Centre for the Arts.

2 Check out the mural on the wall of the Flatiron Building, then cross Church Street and continue to St. Lawrence Market.

3 After exploring the market, turn right down Jarvis Street, then go left to walk along The Esplanade alongside David Crombie Park.

4 At the end, go forward into Parliament Square park (a plaque relates to the site of the first parliament buildings), then cross Parliament Street and walk along Mill Street. Turn right to explore the Distillery Historic District.

8 Reach Jarvis Street, cross diagonally and enter St. James Park to see the Cathedral Church of St. James (1844), once the city's tallest building. Opposite, across King Street, is Toronto Sculpture Garden.

7 Turn right here, and go up Frederick Street into the Old Town Heritage Area, site of the original settlement. At the end of Frederick Street turn left on Adelaide, passing Toronto's First Post Office.

6 Continue west across several intersections, passing the Imperial Oil Opera Theatre (note the mural on the Toronto Sun building opposite) and the Lorraine Kimsa Theatre for Young People.

5 Exit the Distillery site onto Mill Street, cross and walk north on Trinity Street, passing Trinity Studio. Turn left onto Front Street, with distant views of the downtown skyscrapers.

Shopping

ARTS ON KING

This store displays hand-made Canadian crafts from every corner of the nation—glass, paintings, jewelry and ceramics.
➕ N7 ✉ 169 King Street East at Jarvis ☎ 416/777-9617 🚋 King

THE BAY

Designer boutiques and a pleasant store to shop in.
➕ M6 ✉ 176 Yonge at Queen ☎ 416/861-9111 🚋 Queen

BROOKFIELD PLACE

Formerly known as BCE Place, this is worth a visit just to walk through the stunning Allen Lambert Galleria. It's home to about 30 stores and services (and the Hockey Hall of Fame), and links to Union Station, the Air Canada Centre and the PATH system.
➕ M7 ✉ 181 Bay Street ☎ 416/777-6480 🚋 Union

BULLOCH TAILORS

This is where the city's professional, political and military men come to be kitted out. Bespoke suits begin at $995.
➕ M7 ✉ 43 Colborne Street ☎ 416/367-1084 🚋 King

COLLEGE PARK & ATRIUM ON BAY

The first is a more intimate, less hectic version of Eaton Centre, with 100 stores; the second is smaller, with 60 stores.
➕ M4 🚋 College
➕ M5 🚋 Dundas

CORKTOWN DESIGN

Within the Distillery Historic District, this store sells stunning unique items of jewelry from more than 50 contemporary Canadian and international artists.
➕ Q7 ✉ Building 54, 55 Mill Street ☎ 416/861-3020 🚋 King Street East streetcar

DANIEL ET DANIEL

All kinds of foods—from a cappuccino and croissant for breakfast to pâtés, mini-pizzas, quiches, salads and hot-and-cold

CANADA'S OWN

Check out current Canadian fashion talent by visiting Eaton's and the Bay, where they are grouped together. Also cruise through Holt Renfrew. In the Bloor-Yorkville area you'll find Canada's best-known designers: Vivian Shyu, for sophisticated but simple women's fashion; Linda Lundstrom for her easy-to-wear casual, but dressy, separates and outerwear; and Peachy Fresh, a designer's collective. Queen Street West is the domain of young designers: John Fluevog (shoes); Kingi Carpenter (groovy, hip fashions); Kendra Francis at Franke (smooth, cutting-edge nightlife outfits); Lowon Pope (sexy, fun and fanciful); Brian Bailey (imaginative urban chic); and Price Rowan (glamorous and dramatic).

hors d'oeuvres for lunch.
➕ P4 ✉ 248 Carlton Street ☎ 416/968-9275 🚋 College Street East streetcar

EATON CENTRE

A million visitors a week shop in this vast indoor mall on three levels (▷ 52).
➕ M5–M6 ✉ Yonge between Dundas and Queen 🚋 Dundas or Queen

FIRST CANADIAN PLACE

At the base of this towering office complex a gleaming three-level mall has around 120 stores.
➕ L6–L7 ✉ 100 King Street West ☎ 416/862-3138 🚋 King

GEORGE BOURIDIS

Toronto's premier shirt-maker stocks more than 400 fabrics from all over the world. Custom-made shirts start at $250; a silk blouse will set you back at least $260.
➕ M5 ✉ 193 Church Street between Dundas and Shuter Street ☎ 416/363-4868 🚋 Dundas

NICHOLAS HOARE BOOKSHOP

A store that invites browsing, especially for the latest British publications. The staff love books and can answer every question. There's a fireplace and comfy sofa.
➕ M7 ✉ 45 Front Street East ☎ 416/777-2665 🚋 Union

Entertainment and Nightlife

AIR CANADA CENTRE
www.theaircanadacentre.com
Principally the home of the Toronto Maple Leafs hockey team, this also stages superstar concerts.
➕ L8 ✉ 40 Bay Street
☎ 416/815-5500 🚇 Union

BERKELEY STREET THEATRE
www.canstage.com
In a converted historic building, this is one of the theaters of the Canadian Stage Company.
➕ P7 ✉ 26 Berkeley Street
☎ 416/367-8243 🚇 King Street East

CANON THEATRE
The Canon stages high-profile productions, with the Canadian premiere of the musical *We Will Rock You* opening in 2008.
➕ M5 ✉ 244 Victoria Street
☎ 416/872-1212 TicketKing
🚇 Dundas or Queen

C'EST WHAT
A comfortable cellar-style bar for quiet conversation and folk-acoustic music.
➕ M7 ✉ 67 Front Street East ☎ 416/867-9499
🚇 Union

COURT HOUSE CHAMBER LOUNGE
This celebrity favorite has 9m (30ft) ceilings and vintage mirrors, and spins the best of the 1980s and 90s for a hip 25-plus crowd.
➕ M6 ✉ 57 Adelaide Street East ☎ 416/214-9379
🚇 King

ELGIN AND WINTER GARDEN THEATRES
www.heritagefdn.on.ca
A National Historic Site owned by the Ontario Heritage Trust, this is the only double-decker theater still in existence. It is worth a visit just to see the restoration. If you can't get tickets, take a guided tour.
➕ M6 ✉ 189 Yonge Street
☎ 416/314-2901 🚇 Queen

FOUR SEASONS CENTRE FOR THE PERFORMING ARTS
www.fourseasonscentre.ca
Opened in 2006 as the home of the Canadian Opera Company and the National Ballet of Canada, this magnificent theater has the latest technological and acoustic features.

DISTILLERY ARTS

The Distillery Historic District is a cultural center housing professional theater and dance companies, including the acclaimed Soulpepper Theatre Company, Native Earth Performing Arts, Tapestry New Opera Works, DanceWork, Volcano, Tapestry New Opera Works, Nightwood Theatre and the Necessary Angel Theatre Company. The complex also includes a theater museum, a performing arts college and the superb **Young Centre for the Performing Arts** (✉ Buildings 49 and 50 ☎ 416/866-8666).

➕ L6 ✉ 145 Queen Street West ☎ 416/363-6671
🚇 Osgoode

MASSEY HALL
www.roythomson.com
One of the most popular live music venues in the city.
➕ M6 ✉ 178 Victoria Street
☎ 416/872-4255 🚇 Queen

NOW LOUNGE
www.nowtoronto.com/lounge
An interesting program of Canadian and international acts is presented in this intimate little place in the *NOW Magazine* building.
➕ M6 ✉ 189 Church Street
☎ 416/532-7020 🚇 Queen or Dundas

ST. LAWRENCE CENTRE FOR THE ARTS
www.stlc.com
A facility dedicated to providing a high-quality diversity of cultural events.
➕ M7 ✉ 27 Front Street East ☎ 416/366-7723, 1-800/708-6754 box office, 416/366-1656 (admin)
🚇 Union

SONY CENTRE FOR THE PERFORMING ARTS
www.sonycentre.ca
This important venue hosts special big-name concerts, multimedia presentations and short-run shows. A major redevelopment is scheduled to begin June 2008.
➕ M7 ✉ 1 Front Street East
☎ 416/393-7469 🚇 Union

Restaurants

PRICES

Prices are approximate, based on a 3-course meal for one person.

$$$$	over $80
$$$	$60–$80
$$	$35–$60
$	under $35

BB33 ($$)

www.bb33.ca

The bistro is the more formal choice for dinner, with dishes such as braised venison osso buco or duck with cinnamon and raisin couscous. The brasserie has great buffets and a good à la carte menu.

➕ L4 ✉ 33 Gerrard Street West ☎ 416/585-4319 ◉ Bistro: Mon–Sat 5–10pm; Brasserie: Mon–Sat 7–11am, 12–2, 5–9.30, Sun 12–2 (brunch) 🚇 Dundas or College

BYMARK ($$$$)

www.bymark.ca

Dramatic decor of wood, glass and water with a delectable menu of classics and service to match. A bar one floor up offers extreme comfort and views. Summer patio.

➕ L7 ✉ 66 Wellington Street West ☎ 416/777-1144 ◉ Lunch Mon–Fri; dinner Mon–Sat 🚇 Union

CANOE ($$$$)

www.canoerestaurant.com

On the 54th floor of the TDC building. Inventive cuisine making use of Canadian ingredients

(Digby scallops, Alberta beef, Grandview venison).

➕ L7 ✉ 66 Wellington Street West ☎ 416/364-0054 ◉ Lunch and dinner Mon–Fri 🚇 Union

ESPLANADE BIER MARKT ($$)

www.thebiermarkt.com

A traditional Belgian-themed tile, wood and brick bistro where mussels and French fries are king. More than 100 bottled beers and more on tap.

➕ P7 ✉ 58 The Esplanade ☎ 416/862-7575 ◉ Mon–Wed 11am–1am, Thu–Fri 11am–2am, Sat noon–2am, Sun 5–12 🚇 Union

FRAN'S ($)

A massive menu and 24-hour opening makes for a real downtown

pleaser. There are two dozen or more breakfast choices, plus soups, salads, sandwiches, burgers, steak, ribs, chicken, seafood, pasta, fajitas and classic comfort food.

➕ M5 ✉ 200 Victoria Street ☎ 416/932-9867 ◉ 24 hours 🚇 Queen or Dundas

IRISH EMBASSY PUB AND GRILL ($)

www.irishembassypub.com

Upscale to suit the splendid old bank building it occupies, this place is renowned for its food, from hot breakfasts, through lunchtime sandwiches and bar snacks to the entrées you'd expect, including Irish stew and Kilkenny battered haddock with fries.

➕ M7 ✉ 49 Yonge Street ☎ 416/866-8282 ◉ Mon–Fri 11.30am–2am, Sat–Sun 11am–2am 🚇 King

NAMI ($$)

Ultrastylish and very expensive, this is frequented by Japanese business people and their guests. Prime attractions are the really fresh sushi and sashimi and darkly sophisticated interior.

➕ M6 ✉ 55 Adelaide Street East ☎ 416/362-7373 ◉ Lunch Mon–Fri; dinner Mon–Sat 🚇 Queen or King

RICHTREE MARKET ($)

www.richtree.ca

A vast indoor European market with the world's foods made to order at

the cooking stations. There's an in-house bakery, too. Fill up your tray and dine in any one of seven themed areas.  M7 ✉ 42 Yonge Street, in BCE Place ☎ 416/366-8986 ⏰ Breakfast, lunch and dinner daily 🚇 Union

RUTH'S CHRIS STEAK HOUSE ($$$)

www.ruthschris-toronto.com
Early dinners and proximity to theaters and other entertainment make this an ideal choice for pre-show meals. In addition to the steaks, there are seafood, chicken and other choices. ➕ L6 ✉ 145 Richmond Street West ☎ 416/955-1455 or 1-800/544-0808 ⏰ Daily 4.30–10pm (10.45 Fri and Sat) 🚇 Osgoode

SAVOY BISTRO ($$)

www.thesavoy.ca
This is a chic environment in which to enjoy reasonably priced bistro food. Starters such as paté or charcuterie can be followed by steak frites, chicken roulade or rainbow trout nicoise. There's a good cocktail list and pre-show dinners are available from 5pm. The three levels, including an entertainment lounge, finish with a rooftop patio. ➕ M5 ✉ 253 Victoria Street ☎ 416/364-1013 ⏰ Dinner Tue–Sat 🚇 Dundas

SENATOR ($–$$)

www.thesenator.com
Claiming to be the city's oldest restaurant, the Senator is in a fine old building and offers good-value comfort food, such as home-made meat loaf with mashed potatoes, liver and onions, and fish-and-chips. ➕ M5 ✉ 249 Victoria Street ☎ 416/364-3784 ⏰ Lunch Tue–Fri, dinner Tue–Sun 🚇 Dundas

EATON CENTRE EATING

Shopping mall eating conjures up fluorescent-lit food courts, meals in a bag and paper cups of coffee, but in the Eaton Centre you can do much better. Try **Baton Rouge**, justly famous for its succulent ribs, with intimate booths and tables and subdued lighting (✉ Street level ☎ 416/593-9667); the **City Grill**, a cosmopolitan spot with a long menu of sandwiches, quesadillas, salads, pizza, pasta, noodles and main courses such as maple-glazed salmon and pot roast (✉ Level 3 ☎ 416/596-4454); or **Mr Greenjeans**, with a huge menu that includes good-value lunch combos and main courses such as pork tenderloin encrusted in mustard seeds (✉ Level 2 ☎ 416/979-1212). Before you rule out the food court, it does contain the **Original Soup Man**, the New York branch of which was made famous in an episode of *Seinfeld*.

STARFISH ($$)

www.starfishoysterbed.com
The owner of this comfy restaurant is a walking encyclopedia of seafood lore. The array of oysters, oven-roasted black cod and east coast lobsters are tempting. ➕ N6 ✉ 100 Adelaide Street East ☎ 416/366-7827 ⏰ Lunch Mon–Fri; dinner Mon–Sat 🚇 King

SULTAN'S TENT AND CAFÉ MOROC ($$)

www.thesultanstent.com
With a sumptuous tented interior, the restaurant offers delicious and beautifully presented Moroccan food, including tender tagines and couscous dishes. The fixed-price four-course meals are excellent value, and nightly belly-dancing shows are a bonus. ➕ M7 ✉ 49 Front Street East ☎ 416/961-0601 ⏰ Lunch Mon–Fri, dinner Fri–Sat 🚇 Union

TUNDRA ($$$)

Well-named for its focus on Canadian cuisine and wines, even the decor evokes the barren north. The dinner menu might include such dishes as pan-seared striped bass and butter-poached Nova Scotia lobster crumble, or honey bourbon barbecued Cornish hen. ➕ L6 ✉ Hilton Hotel, 145 Richmond Street West ☎ 416/860-6800 ⏰ Breakfast, lunch and dinner daily 🚇 Osgoode

This is where Toronto relaxes—the south-facing strip alongside Lake Ontario. There are parks, traffic-free paths for walking, cycling and roller-blading, open-air stages, and restaurants. The water is busy with kayaks, sailboats and ferries to the islands.

G

Bathurst
Fleet
LAKE SHORE BOULEVARD WEST
Bathurst
Quay
Street
Queens Quay West
Eireann Quay

Toronto City Centre
Airport Ferry

Little Norway
Park

H

Lakeshore

Canadian Wheat Grain Elevator

Spadina Quay Marina

Toronto Music Gardens

parks and Gardens

61

FREDERICK G. GARDINER EXPRESSWAY

Queens
Quay
West

Spadina

Spadina Avenue Slip

0 ——— 250 m
0 ——— 250 yds

J

Peter Street Slip

N

H₂O Park

Rees Street Slip

K

HARBOURFRONT

Maple Leaf Quay
John Quay

The Pier Waterfront Museum

Simcoe Street Slip

Ann Tindall Park

Concert Stage

Harbourfront Centre

York Quay Centre

DuMaurier Theatre

Premiere Dance Theatre
Queens Quay Terminal

Rees

Simcoe

Queens

York

Brennen Boulevard

L

Queens Quay West

YORK STREET

Harbour
Quay

HARBOUR

STREET

Harbour Square

Harbour Square Park

Harbour Commission

Sears Theatre

Air Canada Centre

BAY STREET

M

Toronto Islands

Toronto Island Ferry Terminal

Conference Centre

Queens
YONGE STREET

Freeland Street

LAKE SHORE BOULEVARD EAST

N

Redpath Sugar Museum

Cooper Street

Queens Quay East

Quay

Queens Quay Market

Tate & Lyle Sugar Plant

East

9

8

7

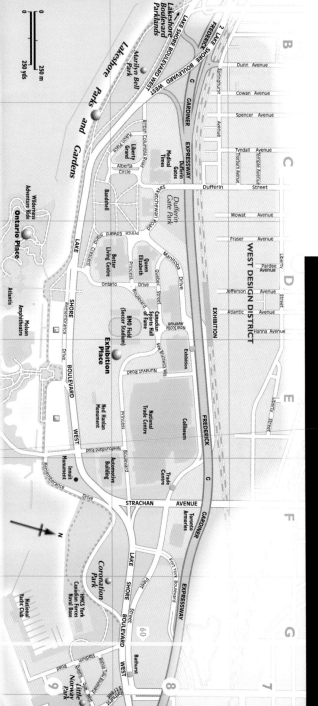

Lakeshore and Islands

Lakeshore Parks and Gardens

Lakeshore Boulevard Parklands

Marilyn Bell Park

Ontario Place
Wilderness Adventure Ride

Atlantis

Molson Amphitheatre

LAKE SHORE BOULEVARD WEST

FREDERICK G LAKE SHORE BOULEVARD 2

GARDINER EXPRESSWAY

British Columbia Road
Liberty Grand
Alberta Circle

Bandshell

Prince Edward Drive
Ontario Drive
Better Living Centre

Saskatchewan Road

Manitoba Drive
Quebec Street
Princess Boulevard Drive

Queen Elizabeth
BMO Field (Soccer Stadium)
Canadian Sports Hall of Fame

Exhibition Place

Medieval Times
Dufferin Gates
Dufferin Gate Park

Dunn Avenue
Cowan Avenue
Spencer Avenue
Tyndall Avenue
Thorburn Avenue
Temple Avenue

Dufferin Street

Mowat Avenue
Fraser Avenue
Liberty
Pardee Avenue
Jefferson Avenue
Atlantic Avenue
Hanna Avenue

Liberty Street

B
C
WEST DESIGN DISTRICT
D
EXHIBITION

Nova Scotia Avenue
New Brunswick Way
Nunavut Road

Ned Hanlan Monument

National Trade Centre
Coliseum

Exhibition

Princess Boulevard

Newfoundland Road
Automotive Building
Trade Centre

Inuit Monument

LAKE SHORE BOULEVARD WEST

Remembrance Drive
Remembrance Drive

STRACHAN AVENUE
Toronto Armories

FREDERICK G GARDINER EXPRESSWAY

Fort York Boulevard

Coronation Park
HMCS York Canadian Forces Naval Base

National Yacht Club

LAKE SHORE BOULEVARD WEST
Fleet Street
Bathurst Street
60

Little Norway Park
Stadium Road
Dan Leckie Way

N

0   250 m
0   250 yds

7
8
9
E
F
G

Harbourfront Centre   TOP 25

● Shopping at Queen's Quay
● Art exhibits at the Power Plant and York Quay Centre
● Craft Studio
● Performances
● Free weekend festivals
● International Marketplace

TIPS

● Winter is just as much fun at Harbourfront, including a large outdoor skating rink.
● Harbourfront Centre is on the Waterfront Trail.

This development is a wonderful example of a waterfront park that is not simply a glorified shopping mall. It's a place to spend the whole day—biking, sailing, canoeing, picnicking, watching crafts-people—and even shopping.

Lakefront leisure Start at Queen's Quay (▷ 69) where, in an old warehouse building, there is an attractive shopping mall with specialty shops. Several restaurants have outside dining areas from which to enjoy the waterfront. Take the lakeside walking trail to York Quay, stopping en route at the Power Plant, a contemporary art gallery, and the Enwave Theatre behind it. On York Quay you'll find artisans glass-making, pot-throwing, jewelry-making, silk-screening or metal-sculpting. You can purchase the results in the adjacent store. York

Clockwise from left: Queen's Quay Terminal interior and exterior; the Du Maurier Theatre; York Quay Centre, exterior and interior views

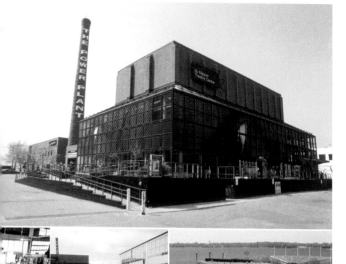

Quay's lakefront has a small pond, a children's play area and the outdoor Sirius Stage. Across the footbridge is John Quay, with several restaurants.

The place to rent a boat In good weather, Harbourfront is a good place to relax on the grass or people-watch from one of the waterfront cafés. Alternatively, sail- and powerboats can be rented or you can sign up for sailing lessons at Queen's Quay Sailing and Powerboating (tel 416/203-3000).

Festivals and events Harbourfront holds more than 4,000 events of all sorts, from the Milk International Children's Festival of music, dance, theater and puppetry, to the International Festival of Authors in October or the First Night Celebration of the Arts in December.

THE BASICS

www.harbourfrontcentre. com

✚ L9

✉ Harbourfront Centre, 235 Queen's Quay West

☎ 416/973-4000

🕐 York Quay Centre daily 10am–11pm (to 9pm Sun). Queen's Quay Wed–Sat 10–9, Sun–Tue 10–6

🍴 Several

🚊 510 streetcar from Union

♿ Very good

💵 Free

❓ Many special events (information at York Quay)

Ontario Place

- Soak City
- Adventure Island
- Wilderness Adventure Ride
F/X Adventure Theatre
- Festival of Fire

TIPS

- If you plan to get an all-day pass, it's cheaper online.
- The free shuttle bus from Union Station can't take strollers or wheelchairs.

This waterfront recreation complex, a futuristic-looking creation of the 1970s, boasts rides, activities and attractions aimed at visitors of all ages.

Always up-to-date Ontario Place is spread over three artificial islands adding up to a 38ha (96-acre) park with rides, attractions, top performers, IMAX films, stage shows and restaurants. The original Ontario Place was built in 1971, but attractions are added each year.

Rides galore The place caters to kids with many imaginative "play" stations. The H2O Generation Station is a huge soft-play climbing structure; the Atom Blaster is a unique foam ball free-for-all. There are thrill rides for the older kids: For dare-devils there is the Hydrofuge, a tubular waterslide

Crowds are attracted by the entertainment and activities at Ontario Place

that sends riders speeding at 50kph (30mph) into a spinning bowl before depositing them into a 2m (6ft) deep pool. The two waterslides, the Pink Twister and the Purple Pipeline, are very popular, as is the flume called Wilderness Adventure Ride. You can shoot the rapids on the Rush River attraction or enjoy the F/X Adventure Theatre, a 30-seat motion simulator showing "Ecozone"—a view of the planet through the eyes of various animals.

Entertainment too Other attractions are inside steel and glass structures—"pods"—where special exhibitions are installed. The Thrill Zone Pod offers the latest simulator experiences and video games. The Molson Amphitheatre seats 16,000 (including 7,000 on the lawns) for summer performances. The Atlantis Complex contains several restaurants and lounges, and an evening dance club.

THE BASICS

www.ontarioplace.com

⊞ D9

✉ 955 Lake Shore Boulevard West

☎ 416/314-9900

🕐 Jul-end Aug daily 10–8; Jun 10–5 (Waterpark 12–4); May and Sep Sat–Sun 10–8

🍽 Many options

🚋 Streetcar 509 or 511 Bathurst to Exhibition, then walk south

🚻 Good

💲 Expensive. Parking is extra and expensive

❓ Special events, including fireworks

HIGHLIGHTS

- Sandy beaches
- Centre Island
- Hanlan's Point
- View from Algonquin Island

TIPS

- If you're planning a picnic, don't bring alcohol—you need to order it in advance and pick it up from Centreville Catering (☎ 416/203-0405).
- Barbecue pits are available, but it's best to bring a portable charcoal barbecue in case they are all taken.

A mere 15-minute ferry ride takes you to this peaceful archipelago with meandering waterways, cycle paths and bucolic lanes, which seems light years away from the bustling city you left behind.

A city retreat Originally a peninsula, shattered by a storm in 1858, the 14 Toronto Islands incorporate 243ha (600 acres) laced with waterways and inlets. People come to walk, cycle, play tennis, feed the ducks, picnic, sit on the beach or go boating. There are swimming areas on Centre and Ward's Island (and a "clothing optional" beach at Hanlan's Point) but they are often polluted.

The main areas These are Centre Island, Ward's Island and Hanlan's Point. The first is the busiest, with Centreville—an old-fashioned amusement

Clockwise from left: Centreville amusement on Centre Island; Toronto's marina and the small Hanlan's Point; a ferry arriving at the Toronto Island docks; Canada geese on the islands; Hanlan's Point

park with an 1890s carousel, a flume ride and antique cars—and a small working farm where children can pet the lambs and ride the ponies. From Centre Island a bridge crosses over the main watercourse (with boats for rent) to the arc of the former peninsula, with Ward's Island to the east and Hanlan's Point to the west. There are sandy beaches all the way round the outer edge and a central pier juts out into the lake. Behind the beaches pathways crisscross lawns dotted with trees, and there are barbecue pits, picnic tables and a kids' playground. Another big attraction for children is the delightful Franklin Children's Garden. Ward's Island is the main residential spot, while the western area includes the Gibraltar Point Lighthouse, Gibraltar Point Centre for the Arts and—closest to the mainland—the City Airport. To explore, rent a bike or take the Island Tram Tour.

THE BASICS

➕ Off map south of harbor. Ferries M9
☎ Centreville 416/203-0405. Ferry 416/392-8193
🍴 Several options
🚍 Harbourfront LRT or Bay 6 and Spadina 77B buses to Ferry Docks
⛴ Approximately every 15 minutes in summer but less frequently in winter
♿ Few
💲 Ferry moderate
❓ Seasonal events

67

More to See

EXHIBITION PLACE

www.explace.on.ca

This huge site includes the National Trade Centre, BMO Field (the 20,000-seat national soccer stadium), RICOH Coliseum (home of the Toronto Marlies hockey team), Canada's Sport Hall of Fame, the Horse Palace riding academy and Toronto's renewable energy cooperative (its wind turbine is an elegant landmark).

There's plenty going on year-round, but the highlight is the annual Canadian National Exhibition from mid-August to early September. It's massive—one of the largest, if not the largest event of its kind in North America and includes exhibitors, attractions, midway rides, dog and horse shows, live performances, a three-day air show and plenty of shopping and food stands. 2008 marks its 130th anniversary.

➕ E8 ✉ Off Lake Shore Boulevard, Strachan Avenue and Dufferin Street ☎ 416/393-6300 (Canadian National Exhibition only) 🚌 509, 511 🚇 Exhibition

LAKESHORE PARKS AND GARDENS

www.toronto.ca/parks

Once a derelict industrial area, the lakeshore has come alive over the last three decades as the resort area of the city. Between the malls, entertainment venues, hotels and marinas a number of green spaces have been created to enhance the waterfront experience. They are all on the Martin Goodman Trail, the Toronto section of the Waterfront Trail, which stretches for 900km (558 miles) along Lake Ontario. The newest park is H2O Park, which opened in June 2007 and was instantly popular, not least for its sandy beach dotted with umbrellas.

A short walk to the west is the unique 0.8ha (2-acre) Toronto Musical Gardens, where the design concept, a collaboration between landscaper Julie Moir Messervy and cellist Yo Yo Ma, was to represent Bach's *First Suite for Unaccompanied Cello*. Areas convey the movements of the piece and free concerts are staged here in summer.

The Canadian National Exhibition

Queen's Quay West

Next is Little Norway Park, a small area west of the grain elevator that gives access to the ferry for the City Airport on the Islands, then right at the end of Queen's Quay West the trail goes off-road into the wide expanse of Coronation Park. There's a naval base in one corner and National Yacht Club and Alexandra Yacht Club facilities jut into the lake. The park has picnic areas and three softball pitches. There is also the World War II 50th Anniversary Memorial and some commemorative tree plantings. At the western end is the Inukshuk monument, an Inuit symbol in the shape of a stone man.

From here the trail continues between Ontario Place and Exhibition Place to Marilyn Bell Park, which is named after the swimmer who in 1954, at the age of 16, became the first person to swim across the lake from New York State. It has a few sports facilities and the Argonaut Rowing Club. The park blends into the Lakeshore Boulevard Parklands, where locals walk their dogs or play tennis.
➕ C9 ☎ 416/392-1111 🚌 509, 510

QUEEN'S QUAY WEST

Stretching from the bottom of Bay Street west to the foot of Bathurst, Queen's Quay West has become one of the city's hotspots. In addition to giving access to attractions such as the Harbourfront Centre (▷ 62–63) and several waterfront parks, it is lined by restaurants, hotels, and good specialty stores and malls. A number of high-rise condo buildings here form some of the hottest real estate in the city.
➕ L9

REDPATH SUGAR MUSEUM

www.redpathsugars.com/museum
If you have a half-hour or so to spare, this unusual little museum tells the story of the company that has refined and sold sugar and sugar products in Canada since 1853. It has displays about sugarcane, sugar beet, refining methods, the slave trade and social aspects of sugar.
➕ M8 ✉ 95 Queen's Quay East
☎ 416/933-8341 🕐 Mon–Fri 10–12, 1–3.30
✋ Free 🚇 Union Station 🚌 6, 97B
(limited services) ♿ Good

★

Toronto Musical Gardens

An Island Stroll

Take a ferry ride to discover an offshore haven, with parkland and beaches, bikes and boating, and spectacular views of the city.

DISTANCE: 2.5km (1.5 miles) **ALLOW:** 3 hours

START

TORONTO ISLANDS PIER
✚ M9 🚏 Pier area

❶ From the Toronto Islands Ferry Terminal take the ferry to Centre Island. Cross the square to the island information booth in the far left corner then go left on the path that leads past Centreville to the bridge.

❷ Cross the bridge and go forward past the fountain, through the gardens to the beach and pier for a look southward over the lake.

❸ Retrace your steps to the fountain, then turn right and follow the path to the boathouse. Loop around the back of the boathouse and continue to the pretty little church of St. Andrews by the Lake.

❹ Continue on the same path, with occasional spectacular views across the water to the downtown sky-scrapers. Later pass the bridge (on your left) to Algonquin Island.

END

TORONTO ISLANDS PIER
✚ M9 🚏 Pier area

❽ As an alternative, from Ward's Island Beach you can turn right onto the boardwalk, which will take you back to the pier area.

❼ From here you can take a ferry back to Centre Island and/or the mainland.

❻ Turn left and follow the path behind the beach, turning left at the end to loop around the residential area, then back along the northern shore to the Ward's Island Ferry Dock.

❺ Walk past the Island Canoe Club building, then turn right to Ward's Island Beach.

WALK

LAKESHORE AND ISLANDS

Shopping

BOUNTY
Within the York Quay Centre, part of the Harbourfront Centre, this is a terrific crafts shop showcasing contemporary Canadian works. These include pieces made by the center's resident artists, who can often be seen at work in the studios here.
➕ L9 ✉ 236 Queens Quay West ☎ 416/973-4993 🕐 Daily 11–6 (to 8pm Thu and Fri) Ⓤ Union then LRT

INTERNATIONAL MARKETPLACE
Stands selling crafts, jewelry, textiles and other goods from all over the world are set up on one of the quays at the Harbourfront Centre every summer weekend.
➕ L9 ☎ 416/973-4000 Ⓤ Union then LRT

KITCHEN TABLE
If you are looking for picnic supplies to take to the islands or one of the lakeshore parks, look no farther than this store with bakery and deli goods and fresh fruit.
➕ L8 ✉ 12 Queen's Quay West ☎ 416/777-9874 🕐 Daily 6am–midnight Ⓤ Union then LRT

LCBO
The Liquor Control Board of Ontario store has a great selection of wines, including Canadian varieties, beers that are kept in a cold room, spirits and the fixings for cocktails.
➕ M8 ✉ 2 Cooper Street, Queen's Quay ☎ 416/864-6863 🕐 Mon–Sat 9am–10pm, Sun 12–6

QUEEN'S QUAY TERMINAL
This upscale mall is a glittering space right on the lakeshore with an interesting selection of stores, including fashions, homewares, crafts, perfumes, toys, jewelry. Standouts include the Arctic Nunavut store, with goods ranging from musk ox leather items to children's books and Taluq crafts, and the Museum of Inuit Art, with crafts for sale. There are several

THE TILLEY STORY
All Alex Tilley wanted was a decent, good-quality cotton hat to wear on fishing trips. It turned out that he had to invent one himself. It found such favor with anglers and outdoorsmen everywhere that over the last couple of decades the business has grown into an international success. In addition to the six stores in Toronto, Montréal, Mississauga and Vancouver, Tilley supplies retailers throughout Canada, the US, Europe, Australasia, Japan, Singapore and the Turks and Caicos Islands. The range now includes all kinds of outdoor and travel clothing and accessories. For more information, see www.tilley.com.

good restaurants with lakefront patios.
➕ L9 ✉ 207 Queen's Quay West ☎ 416/203-0510 🕐 Wed–Sat 10–9, Sun–Tue 10–6 (hours may change seasonally) Ⓤ Union then LRT 🚇 Spadina then LRT

TILLEY ENDURABLES
This store bears the name of the man who developed the famous "Tilley Hat," which can be used for a variety of purposes in the wilderness. The store also stocks other great outdoors gear, including lightweight underwear, waterproofs and a multipocketed jacket that is invaluable for photographers. The larger, flagship store is on Don Mills Road.
➕ J9 ✉ 207 Queen's Quay West ☎ 416/203-0463 Ⓤ Union then LRT ✉ 900 Don Mills Road ☎ 416/441-6141

WHEEL EXCITEMENT
OK, it is not a store as such, but if you've watched the rollerbladers and cyclists zipping along the lakeshore routes and want to have a try, this is the place to rent the equipment. They have inline skates, mountain bikes and adult tricycles by the hour or the day, plus lessons. New and used equipment is sold off in the fall.
➕ K9 ✉ 249 Queen's Quay West, Unit 110 ☎ 416/260-9000 🕐 Call for details Ⓤ Union, then LRT

Entertainment and Nightlife

BMO FIELD

It's a new venue in the city, but quickly made its mark with the first Genesis tour in 15 years, which played at the stadium on September 7, 2007. No doubt there will be more.

➕ D8 ⊠ Exhibition Place ☎ 416/360-4625 🚌 509, 511 🚊 Exhibition

CINESPHERE

This was the first permanent IMAX theater in the world and still has the largest screen in the Greater Toronto Area. It has a long list of IMAX format movies, and also shows some regular feature films. You have to pay at least the grounds-only admission to Ontario Place to see a movie here, but the experience is worth it.

➕ D9 ⊠ Ontario Place, 990 Lakeshore Boulevard West ☎ 416/314-9900, 416/870-8000 Ticketmaster 🚌 509, 511 🚊 Exhibition

HARBOURFRONT CENTRE

www.harbourfrontcentre.com This excellent not-for-profit arts and entertainment center (▷ 62–63) has events year-round, including concerts, dance, drama and festivals. It attracts performers and art forms that might not normally be seen in commercial venues, with a strong program of world music. The center's theaters include The Premiere Dance Theatre, which hosts a world-famous contemporary dance season and other events; the Enwave Theatre puts on a variety of concerts, world music and dance; the Studio Theatre has drama, kids' workshop productions and other events. There are also two open-air venues, the Sirius Stage, with an eclectic program of concerts, cabaret and comedy, and the Toronto Musical Gardens (▷ 68).

➕ K9–L9 ⊠ 235 Queen's Quay West ☎ 416/973-4000 box office, 416/973-4600 admin 🚊 Union then LRT

STREET MUSIC

When the weather is suitable, there's nothing Canadians like more than to be outside, and that applies to many of their musicians, too. There are plenty of organized open-air concerts, with the Harbourfront Centre, Dundas Square and the Distillery Historic District among popular venues, and you might even see one of the big-name local bands playing on a makeshift stage on a city square (particularly if they have a cause to support). Equally appealing (usually) are the casual street musicians you find unexpectedly—anything from a guy with a guitar to a classical string quartet, and you won't use the subway for long before you hear one of the auditioned acts allowed to play down there.

MEDIEVAL TIMES DINNER AND TOURNAMENT

Jousting knights charge toward each other at high speed on Andalucian stallions while diners enjoy a multi-course feast preferred by serving wenches. The knights toss the javelin and wield fierce-looking bola and alabarda.

➕ C8 ⊠ Exhibition Place, Lakeshore Boulevard ☎ 416/260-1234 or 1-888/935-6878 🚌 509, 511 streetcars 🚊 Exhibition

POLSON PIER

www.polsonpier.com Located on the water, Polson Pier offers all kinds of nightlife action. Dive into the Deep End Nightclub and you'll see what a million dollars in sight and sound feels and looks like. When you're looking for a party, you'll be sure to find it at Tides Party Bar—billiards and large screen TVs that visually interact with the dance floor. The Aqua Lounge is a more intimate nightclub setting with a separate dance floor and a great Toronto skyline view. Other activities include karting, a golf driving range, volleyball, swimming pool, paintball range, drive-in and more.

➕ Q9 ⊠ 11 Polson Street ☎ 416/469-5655 🚌 72A, 172

Restauraunts

PRICES

Prices are approximate, based on a 3-course meal for one person.

$$$$	over $80
$$$	$60–$80
$$	$35–$60
$	under $35

BOAT HOUSE GRILL ($$)

One of the places with lakefront dining patios, and great views from inside, too. It offers a typical grill menu of steaks, ribs, chicken and seafood, plus pastas, pizzas, stir-fry and jambalaya. There's a good brunch menu.

➕ L9 ✉ Queen's Quay Terminal, Main Level, 207 Queen's Quay West ☎ 416/203-6300 ⏰ Daily 11am–midnight; brunch Sat–Sun and holiday Mon 10.30–3 Ⓜ Union then LRT

CAPTAIN JOHN'S HARBOUR BOAT ($$$)

www.captainjohns.ca
A former Yugoslavian cruise ship now at anchor opposite the bottom of Yonge Street houses this restaurant. The nautical decor features lots of polished brass and wood and the menu focuses on seafood, with a few meat and vegetarian dishes. The Alaskan king crab feast is hard to beat.

➕ M8 ✉ 1 Queen's Quay West, Captain John's Pier ☎ 416/363-6062 ⏰ Mon–Sat 11–11, Sun 10.30am–11pm Ⓜ Union then LRT

COMMODORE'S ($$$$)

There's a spectacular view of the harbor from this fine-dining restaurant, where you might start with a warm duck and mushroom salad or seared East Coast scallops. Entrées include veal with zucchini falafel or paprika-spiced pickerel with warm blue potato and ham hock salad. Menu changes seasonally.

➕ K9 ✉ Radisson Hotel Admiral, 249 Queen's Quay West ☎ 416/203-3333 or 1-888/201-1718 ⏰ Dinner daily Ⓜ Union then LRT

HARBOUR SIXTY STEAK HOUSE ($$$)

www.harboursixty.com
Climb stone steps to a

PICNIC PLACES

With all the parks lining the lake shore, there's no shortage of places to spread a blanket and lay out your feast. Many of the parks have picnic tables, too. Take the ferry over to the Toronto Islands and you will find not only tables, but also barbecue pits, though they get taken very quickly. If you take your own barbecue, only small, charcoal burning types are allowed on the ferry (they won't carry alcohol either). You can get supplies at the excellent Kitchen Table (▷ 71) or from the big Loblaws supermarket on Queen's Quay East.

baroque-inspired foyer to enjoy the finest basic ingredients. Prime beef, tuna, lobsters on ice, Atlantic salmon and the best slow-roasted prime rib beef in town.

➕ L8 ✉ 60 Harbour Street ☎ 416/777-2111 ⏰ Mon–Fri 11.30–5, Sat–Sun 11.30am–1am Ⓜ Union

ISLAND PARADISE RESTAURANT AND CAROUSEL CAFÉ ($)

On Centre Island, this lovely spot has great views of the city. There's plenty of outdoor seating with umbrellas for shade, and a menu that will please the whole family.

➕ Off map ✉ Centreville, Centre Island ☎ 416/203-0405 ⏰ Varies seasonally; call for details 🚢 Centre Island

RECTORY CAFÉ ($–$$)

www.rectorycafe.com
This delightful café is full of character, with the works of local artists on the walls and intimate seating. In good weather head to a table in the garden. The small menu features well-cooked dishes such as PEI mussels or goat cheese salad, followed by salmon, vegetarian risotto and roasted chicken supreme. There are also lunchtime sandwiches.

➕ Off map ✉ 102 Lakeshore Avenue, Ward's Island ☎ 416/203-2152 ⏰ Seasonal hours; call for details 🚢 Ward's Island

Powerhouses of government and learning are concentrated around Queen's Park, between the busy thoroughfares of College and Bloor streets. Farther north, streets of heritage homes fill the Annex, leading to a remarkable piece of architecture.

Queen's Park and Midtown

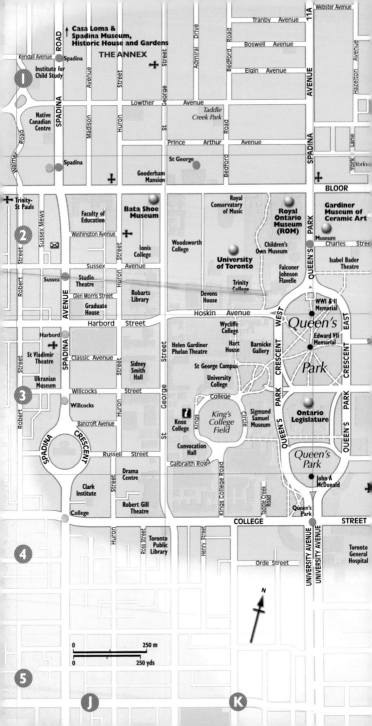

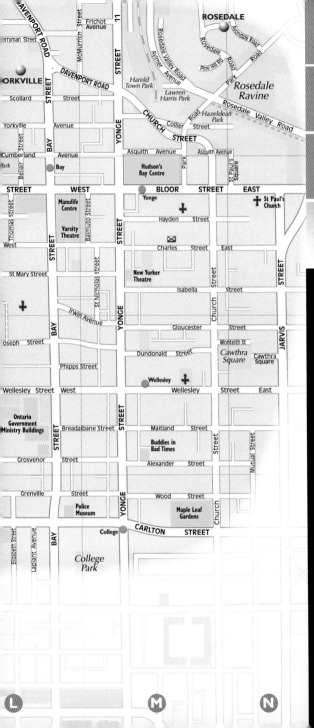

L   M   N

Bata Shoe Museum

HIGHLIGHTS

- Mold of Homo sapiens footprint made 3.7 million years ago
- 4,500-year-old wooden sandals
- 2,000-year-old espadrilles
- 500-year-old footwear of a Mayan boy sacrifice
- 7.5cm (3in) "gin lien" for bound feet

TIP

- Allow more time than you think you are going to need and bring the children—there's lots of fun to be had here.

Imelda Marcos would be in her element at this museum. Housed in a structure resembling a shoe box, there are more than 10,000 items in the displays of footwear past and present.

More than just shoes The main permanent exhibit traces the history of shoes from a footprint made 3.7 million years ago in Tanzania to the extraordinary shoes of today. The sheer variety of beautiful and truly striking footwear is amazing. Each display is set against an appropriate series of cutouts reflecting the particular period or geographic location. There are all kinds of ceremonial shoes: leather sandals with gilded images worn by the King of Kumasi in Ghana for state occasions; wedding shoes from various cultures; and lacquered and painted shoes worn to Shinto shrines

Clockwise from left: the hard-to-miss Bata Shoe Museum; interior staircase; exterior view; a pair of Elton John's shoes; sheepskin boots and moccasins; one of actress Lana Turner's sandals

in Japan. The museum is a gold mine of little-known facts; for instance, that Elizabeth I was in part responsible for the foot problems caused by high heels because she popularized them in an attempt to make herself appear taller. The style was limited to the elite, hence the term "well-heeled." Toe-length was another important indicator of social status; in England, in the mid-14th century, anyone earning less than 40 livres was not allowed to wear pointed toes, a noble-man could wear shoes with toes 69cm (24in) long, and a prince could wear toes of any length.

The Walk of Fame This includes Picasso's mock zebra lace-ups, Elton John's 30cm (12in) high platform shoes, one of John Lennon's "Beatle Boots" from the early 1960s and Marilyn Monroe's red leather pumps.

THE BASICS

www.batashoemuseum.ca

➕ J2

✉ 327 Bloor Street West

☎ 416/979-7799

🕐 Mon–Wed, Fri–Sat 10–5, Thu 10–8, Sun noon–5

🚇 St. George

♿ Excellent

💲 Moderate; free Thu 5–8pm

❓ Lectures, guided tours, family events, folkloric events

Casa Loma

Interior views (below) and looking toward Casa Loma (right)

THE BASICS

www.casaloma.org

➕ Off map at J1

✉ 1 Austin Terrace at Davenport and Spadina Road

☎ 416/923-1171

🕐 House daily 9.30–5; gardens May–end Oct daily 9.30–5. Last admission 4pm

🍴 Café

Ⓜ Dupont

♿ Good

💲 Moderate

❓ Self-guided audio tour; garden talks; special events

HIGHLIGHTS

- Great Hall
- Oak Room
- Conservatory
- View from the towers

TIPS

- Visitors with young children should be prepared to tackle staircases because the elevators can't take strollers.
- There's a charge for parking at Casa Loma.

A mix of 17th-century Scottish baronial and 20th Century Fox, Casa Loma is a rich man's folly. It cost $3.5 million to build, yet after real estate changes, only 10 years later was valued at $27,305.

Splendor Canadian-style A magnificent and whimsical place with its Elizabethan chimneys, Rhenish turrets and secret passageways, Casa Loma is Sir Henry Pellatt's idea of what constituted European aristocratic splendor. Between 1911 and 1914 Pellatt created this fantasy home, importing Scottish stonemasons and Italian woodcarvers, then spending an additional $1.5 million furnishing the 98 rooms. A hammerbeam ceiling covers the 20m (66ft) high Great Hall; three artisans took three years to carve the paneling in the Oak Room; splendid bronze doors lead into the marble conservatory crowned with a stained-glass dome. Modern luxuries included an elevator, a private telephone system, marble swimming pool, 10,000-volume library, 15 baths and 5,000 electric lights. A tunnel runs out to the stables, where the horses, amid Spanish tile and mahogany, had their names displayed in 18-carat gold letters at the head of each stall.

The bubble bursts The son of a stockbroker, Pellatt went into the brokerage business after college, and amassed $17 million. Still in his 20s, he founded Toronto's first hydroelectric power company, but his wealth evaporated in 1920 when electric power was ruled a public utility. Pellatt eventually died penniless in 1939.

Gardiner Museum of Ceramic Art

TOP 25

Ceramic sculptures on display in the museum

THE BASICS

www.gardinermuseum.com
✚ L2
✉ 111 Queen's Park
☎ 416/586-8080
🕐 Mon–Thu 10–6, Fri 10–9, Sat–Sun 10–5
🚇 Museum
♿ Very good
💵 Moderate; free Fri 4–9 and all day first Fri of month
❓ Tours, lectures

HIGHLIGHTS

● Olmec figures
● Smiling figures
● Majolica
● *Commedia dell'arte* figures
● Scent bottles

In 2006 this outstanding museum reopened with an additional area in which to display its internationally significant ceramics collections of nearly 3,000 pieces. These include the Ancient Americas, Chinese, English, Italian, other European, Japanese and contemporary.

Colorful earthenware The marvelous collection of pre-Columbian pottery includes figures and vessels dating from 3000BC to the 16th century AD, ranging from Mexico to Peru. Among them are some remarkable pieces by the Olmecs, red clay Nayarit figures, Zacatecan-style male statuettes with mushroom-shape horns, smiling figures from Nopiloa, Los Cerro, or Isla de Sacrificios, fine orange and plumbate ware of the Mayans, and Aztec objects. The next great period of ceramic art is represented by colorful Italian majolica from the 15th and 16th centuries, and there is a selection of English tin-glazed earthenware, including familiar blue-and-white delftware.

Delicate porcelain The porcelain collection is extraordinary. It includes figures by Meissen's sculptor-potter Joachim Kändler and some prime examples of Sèvres. English porcelain is well represented, from the early softpaste pieces manufactured at Chelsea and Bow to the later bone china that was invented by Josiah Spode. The collection also features 120 figures from the *commedia dell'arte* and 100 mid-18th-century scent bottles, with examples ranging from early Meissen to highly decorated rococo versions from various sources.

Ontario Legislature

Most parliamentary institutions deliver great entertainment, and the Ontario Provincial legislature is no exception, with the 130 members heckling and cheering as they debate and pass laws. The highlight of any day in the chamber is question time.

Parliamentary session In this impressive four-story chamber the laws affecting 9 million Ontarians are passed. On a dais sits the Speaker, who presides over the house. To the right sits the Government; to the left, the Opposition. In the center is the Clerks' table, with the mace. Behind the Clerks' table is a smaller table for Hansard record-keepers. On the steps of the dais sit the Legislative Pages, who run errands in the house. Above the Speaker is the press gallery. Sessions are opened and closed by the Lieutenant Governor representing Queen Elizabeth II.

Architectural and historical grandeur Even if the house is not sitting you can tour the building, a massive Romanesque Revival structure of reddish-brown sandstone, opened in 1893. A grand staircase lined with portraits of Ontario premiers sweeps up to the chamber above. An enormous stained-glass ceiling-window lights the East Wing, where the premier has his office. The west lobby has mosaic floors, and Italian marble columns in the beaux-arts style, with carved capitals. On the ground level are exhibits, including the provincial mace, which was stolen by the Americans during the 1812 War and returned only in 1934.

THE BASICS

www.ontla.on.ca

K3

✉ Queen's Park

☎ 416/325-7500

◐ Victoria Day Weekend–Labour Day daily 9–4; rest of year Mon–Fri 10–4

🍴 Cafeteria

🚇 Queen's Park, Museum

♿ Good

💲 Free

❓ Public gallery viewing when parliament is in session

HIGHLIGHTS

- Chamber of the Legislature
- Question time
- Stained-glass ceiling in the East Wing
- The mace

Royal Ontario Museum

HIGHLIGHTS

- Dinosaurs
- Stair of Wonders
- Spirit House
- China Galleries
- Middle East and South Asia
- The Americas Gallery

TIPS

- Free admission one-and-a half hours before closing (some restrictions) and half-price on Friday after 4.30.
- School groups tend to visit in the morning.

In June 2007 the spectacular opening ceremony for the Michael Lee-Chin Crystal symbolized a new era for what was already Canada's largest museum. The massive enlargement and remodeling of existing galleries should be completed in 2009.

Michael Lee-Chin Crystal Ever controversial, the Crystal literally bursts out of the 94-year-old walls of the original museum in great prisms that tower over Bloor Street, enabling passersby to look up and see exhibits in the halls above. Inside, eight new galleries have crazy angles and sweeping curves and are bathed in natural light. A fine-dining restaurant has incredible views. Threading up through the building is the Stair of Wonders, highlighting the museum's more unusual exhibits.

Clockwise from left: entrance to the museum; a totem inside the museum; a highly decorated ceiling; detail of an arch above the windows at the entrance; bronze seated Buddha on display; outside the gallery

The collections The ROM has almost 6 million objects in its varied collections, which incorporate world cultures and natural history. The Chinese collections are particularly outstanding, and include galleries devoted to temple art, sculpture, decorative arts and other historic objects. Canada is represented in the excellent Sigmund Samuel and Daphne Cockwell galleries, the latter focusing on First Peoples' culture and art. Other exhibitions range from ancient European civilizations to Japanese ceramics.

For children Most popular with children—and many adults—is the world-class collection of dinosaur skeletons and fossils, and the bat exhibit, which includes a walk-through bat cave diorama. Young visitors are also enthralled by the hands-on galleries, including a digital suite.

THE BASICS

www.rom.on.ca

🔾 K2

✉ 100 Queen's Park

☎ 416/586-8000

🕐 Mon–Thu, Sat–Sun 10–5.30, Fri 10–9.30

🍴 Food Studio, C5 Restaurant

🚇 St. George, Museum

♿ Excellent

💲 Expensive

University of Toronto

Exterior (left) and the Great Hall of Hart House (right)

THE BASICS

www.utoronto.ca

K2

West of Queen's Park

416/978-5000

Gallery Grill in Hart House and numerous cafeterias in campus buildings

Museum or Queen's Park

506 streetcar

Good

Free

Tours Jun–Aug

HIGHLIGHTS

- Hart House
- Knox College Circle
- Robarts Library
- Justina M. Barnicke Art Gallery

Important scientific discoveries have been made at this venerable institution, most notably insulin. The university also numbers many world-famous names among its past students and teachers.

Famous alumni and remarkable research

Canada's largest university was founded in 1827. Its scientific achievements include work that led to the development of the chemical laser; the first electronic heart pacemaker; and some ground-breaking discoveries in genetics. Notable alumni include authors Margaret Atwood, Farley Mowat and Stephen Leacock; figures from the movie world Atom Egoyan, Norman Jewison and Donald Sutherland; opera singers Teresa Stratas and Maureen Forrester; and prime ministers Mackenzie King and Lester Pearson.

Gothic and modern

Stroll around the main St. George campus to view the mixture of architecture. On Hoskin Avenue see Wycliffe and Trinity colleges, the first a monument of redbrick Romanesque Revival and the second a Gothic complex with chapel and eye-catching gardens. Around the corner on Devonshire Place, Massey College is a 1960s building. The heart of the university is Hart House, modeled on Magdalen College, Oxford. See the collection of Canadian art in the Justina M. Barnicke Art Gallery in the west wing. South of Hart House is the Romanesque Revival University College, with an arts center in the Laidlaw Building. King's College Circle passes by several other stately university buildings.

More to See

ROSEDALE

Rosedale is Toronto's most affluent neighborhood, with large, beautiful homes owned by the city's movers and shakers. Many of the buildings, which mostly date from the mid-19th century to the 1920s, are listed Heritage Properties, and are set on large, landscaped lots around pleasant leafy streets. It's no accident that some of Toronto's most upscale shopping abuts Rosedale, in the Yorkville area (▷ right). The district makes for a pleasant stroll.

🚩 M1   🚇 Rosedale

SPADINA MUSEUM: HISTORIC HOUSE AND GARDENS

www.toronto.ca/culture/spadina.htm
Just along the road from over-the-top Casa Loma (▷ 80–81), this fine mansion, with its original furnishings and gas lights, was once at the heart of an estate with its own golf course. After an entertaining introductory film, there's an excellent guided tour that really brings the wealthy Austin family to life, with anecdotes and pointers to personal possessions of the family that still dot the rooms. Afterward, you can take a stroll in the lovely gardens.

🚩 Off map at J1   ✉ 285 Spadina Road   ☎ 416/392-6910   🕐 Apr–Labour Day Tue–Sun and holiday Mon 12–5; Sep–Jan Tue–Fri 12–4, Sat–Sun and Thanksgiving Mon noon–5; Jan–Mar Sat–Sun 12–5   🚇 Dupont   ♿ Good   💲 Moderate

YORKVILLE

Once a village outside the city, in the 1960s this became Toronto's very own Haight-Ashbury, frequented by such local talent as Joni Mitchell and Neil Young. Now its leafy cobblestone streets have become the city's most upscale shopping area, with designer boutiques, luxury homewares, antiques and other desirables in the classy Hazelton Lanes mall and along Yorkville Avenue and Bloor and Cumberland streets. The wine festival every May endorses the air of fine living. Try to visit the Village of Yorkville Park, designed to represent geographical elements of southern Ontario.

🚩 L1   🚇 Bloor-Yonge, Bay

A building housing boutiques in the Yorkville District

Spadina House

Midtown Hits

Yet another facet of Toronto: the stately buildings of parliament and academia, the ROM, and upscale shopping in Yorkville.

DISTANCE: 3km (1.8 miles) **ALLOW:** 2 hours

START

ONTARIO PARLIAMENT
✚ L7 🚇 Union Square

END

BLOOR-YONGE
✚ L8 🚇 Queens Park station

1 Turn your back to the facade of the Ontario Provincial Parliament Buildings, walk south to College Street and turn right. At King's College Road take another right and walk through the university campus.

2 Take King's College Circle west to Tower Road. En route, on your left will be University College opposite the Stewart Observatory.

3 Proceed north to Hart House, pause for a meal at the Gallery Grill, and then visit Soldier's Memorial Tower. Turn right along Hoskin Avenue to Trinity College and then walk east toward Queen's Park.

4 Go left on Avenue Road, going north past the Royal Ontario Museum and the Gardiner Museum. Turn right on fashionable Bloor Street, then head left on Yonge Street to Cumberland Street and walk west.

8 Continue to Yonge. Turn right and cross the street to the Metro Library and walk south to the Bloor-Yonge subway stop.

7 Come back out the way you went in and browse through the galleries on Hazelton Avenue. Backtrack to Yorkville Avenue and go left along it to Bay Street; cross Bay. Note the old Firehall and the Yorkville Public Library, both on the left.

6 Cross Yorkville and go down Hazelton Lane to the Hazelton Lanes Complex, where contemporary designer stores can be found, along with the vast Whole Foods Market—a superb organic food emporium.

5 You are now in the trendy shopping area of Yorkville. Turn down Old York Lane to Yorkville Avenue.

WALK

QUEEN'S PARK AND MIDTOWN

88

Shopping

ALL THE BEST FINE FOODS
Breads, salads, entrées, jams, relishes, sauces and cheeses. Take a leaf out of the book of Rosedale's residents.
⊞ K5 ⊠ 1099 Yonge Street
☎ 416/928-3330
🚇 Rosedale

ASHLEY CHINA
It stocks all the great names in china, and in glass (Kosta Boda, Waterford, Baccarat).
⊞ J6 ⊠ 55 Bloor Street West ☎ 416/964-2900
🚇 Bloor-Yonge

L'ATELIER GREGORIAN
This is a store for the devoted music lover. It contains a stunning collection of classical music and jazz CDs.
⊞ J6 ⊠ 70 Yorkville Avenue
☎ 416/922-6477 🚇 Bloor-Yonge

THE DISH COOKING STUDIO
This Yabu Pushelberg-designed studio combines cooking school, café and retail store. The creation of Trish Magwood, host of Food Network's *Party Dish*, you'll find kitchenware, tableware, cookbooks, plus spices, oils, teas and other ingredients.
⊞ H5 ⊠ 390 Dupont Street
☎ 416/920-5559 🚇 Dupont

FIFTY ONE ANTIQUES
Specializes in 17th- and 18th-century furniture (Empire, Biedermeier and other styles), along with various decorative items: vases, lamps, carvings, European paintings and other accessories.
⊞ J6 ⊠ 21 Avenue Road
☎ 416/968-2416 🚇 Bay

GUILD SHOP
A prime place to purchase the latest and best in Canadian crafts by named artists, as well as Inuit and Native Canadian art.
⊞ J6 ⊠ 118 Cumberland Street ☎ 416/921-1721
🚍 Bay

HARRY ROSEN
Three floors of fashions for men, including all the top men's designers—Armani, Valentino, Calvin Klein and Hugo Boss.
⊞ J6 ⊠ 82 Bloor Street West ☎ 416/972-0556
🚇 Bloor-Yonge or Bay

BLOOR/YORKVILLE

This little enclave bordering the elite residential area of Rosedale is the hub of Toronto's upscale shopping, with leafy lanes of fashion boutiques, gourmet food stores and chic interior decor and a clutch of international designer names such as Chanel, Tiffany and Hermès. Hazelton Lanes is the classiest shopping mall in the city. It's a great area for strolling, shopping and celebrity-spotting.

HOLT RENFREW
Canada's answer to Harvey Nichols. Three floors of designer fashion, a hairdressing salon, Estée Lauder Spa, perfumes and a café.
⊞ J6 ⊠ 50 Bloor Street West ☎ 416/922-2333
🚇 Bloor-Yonge

SCIENCE CITY
Here, you will find fossil specimens, chemistry kits, hologram watches and all kinds of science-oriented games and books. For the seriously scientific, the optical instruments, include telescopes.
⊞ J6 ⊠ 50 Bloor Street West in Holt Renfrew Centre
☎ 416/968-2627 🚇 Bloor-Yonge

SILVERBRIDGE
Marvelously sculptured pieces of sterling silver. Necklaces, bracelets, rings and earrings for women, plus cuff links, money clips and key holders for men, all beautifully crafted. Prices range from $60 to $1,600.
⊞ J6 ⊠ 162 Cumberland Street ☎ 416/923-2591
🚍 Bay

STOLLERY'S
Long-established store with a distinct English flavor. Men's and women's clothes from the likes of Austin Reed and Burberry.
⊞ K6 ⊠ 1 Bloor Street West
☎ 416/922-6173 🚇 Bloor-Yonge

Entertainment and Nightlife

AVENUE

Beautiful people, professional hockey players and visiting celebs are four-deep at the bar on weekends. Great Martinis and a good bar menu.
⊞ K1 ✉ Four Seasons Hotel, 21 Avenue Road ☎ 416/964-0411 🚇 Bay

BA BA LÚU

A classy and sophisticated venue in Yorkville that's popular for its salsa dancing and Latin food.
⊞ L1 ✉ 136 Yorkville Avenue, Lower Level ☎ 416/515-0587 🚇 Bay

BUDDIES IN BAD TIMES THEATRE

www.buddiesinbadtimes theatre.com
Not only is this the premier gay theater in Canada, it has also nurtured many contemporary straight writers. On the cutting edge, it delivers theater that challenges social boundaries. Extra draws are Tallulah's Cabaret (very popular Fri and Sat) and the bar.
⊞ M3 ✉ 12 Alexander Street ☎ 416/975-8555 🚇 College, Wellesley

FREETIMES CAFÉ

www.freetimescafe.com
Go to hear the folk acoustic entertainment. Monday is open house, so bring your instrument and sign up at 7pm.
⊞ H4 ✉ 320 College Street between Major and Roberts ☎ 416/967-1078 🚇 College streetcar

HART HOUSE THEATRE

www.harthousetheatre.ca
The performing arts venue of the University of Toronto showcases Canada's talent in a range of productions.
⊞ K3 ✉ 7 Hart House Circle, University of Toronto ☎ 416/978-6880 🚇 Queen's Park, Museum

LEE'S PALACE

www.leespalace.com
Venue for the latest in rock music, including

GAY TORONTO

To get a fix on the scene, pick up *Xtra!* or go to **Gay Liberation Bookstore/Glad Day Bookshop** (⊞ K6 ✉ 598a Yonge Street ☎ 416/961-4161). Also check these websites: www.xtra.ca; www.gaytoronto.com; and www.gaytorontotourism.com. The area around the Church Street and Wellesley Street intersection has joined the ranks of Toronto's "neighborhoods" as the Church & Wellesley Gay Village, with lots of clubs and bars, including **Woody's** (⊞ K7 ✉ 467 Church Street ☎ 416/972-0887; **Slack's** (⊞ M3 ✉ 562 Church Street ☎ 416/928-2151); **Statlers Piano Bar** (⊞ M3 ✉ 487 Church Street ☎ 416/850-1209) and **Crews/Tango/The Zone** (⊞ M3 ✉ 508–510 Church Street ☎ 416/972-1662).

---

up-and-coming British groups. Home to local alternative bands. Dance bar with DJ.
⊞ H2 ✉ 529 Bloor Street West ☎ 416/532-1598 🚇 Bathurst

PEGASUS BAR

This lively place in Toronto's gay village is for everyone, with music and dancing that's less frantic than in the nearby clubs, plus pool and darts, or just enjoying a drink with an eclectic crowd.
⊞ M3 ✉ 489B Church Street ☎ 416/927-8832 🚇 Wellesley

PHOENIX CONCERT THEATRE

Patti Smith, Screaming Headless Torso and Smashing Pumpkins have played here. Dance on weekends in an Egyptian-Greek fantasy set.
⊞ N3 ✉ 410 Sherbourne Street ☎ 416/323-1251 🚇 Wellesley or College

TRANZAC

www.tranzac.org
The Toronto Australia New Zealand Club is a nonprofit venue promoting music, theater and the arts in both the Main Hall and the Southern Cross Lounge. There's something on most evenings, including folk, jazz and indie bands, some with no cover charge.
⊞ H2 ✉ 292 Brunswick Avenue ☎ 416/923-8137 🚇 Spadina

Restaurants

PRICES

Prices are approximate, based on a 3-course meal for one person.

$$$$	over $80
$$$	$60–$80
$$	$35–$60
$	under $35

BISTRO 990 ($–$$)

www.bistro990.ca
Informality and a superi-or kitchen combine to make this one of the hottest tickets in town. Attentive service and the Provençal cuisine favorites explain why.
➕ L3 ✉ 990 Bay Street ☎ 416/921-9990 ⏰ Lunch Mon–Fri; dinner daily
🚇 Wellesley

BLOOR STREET DINER ($)

Serving shoppers and late-nighters, it combines an espresso bar, a rotis-serie where meat and fish are prepared in Provençal style and a café-terrasse in summer.
➕ L2 ✉ 55 Bloor Street West in the Manulife Centre ☎ 416/928-3105 ⏰ Daily 11.30am–1am (until 2am Fri–Sat) 🚇 Bay or Bloor-Yonge

BOBA ($$$)

www.boba.ca
This chic restaurant in a heritage house serves imaginative, healthy food that's full of flavor.
➕ K1 ✉ 90 Avenue Road ☎ 416/961-2622 ⏰ Dinner Mon–Sat 🚇 Bay or St. George

FUTURE BAKERY ($)

European-style stand-in-line cafeteria, beloved for its large portions of goulash, cabbage rolls and schnitzel sandwiches.
➕ H3 ✉ 483 Bloor Street West ☎ 416/922-5875 ⏰ Daily 24 hours 🚇 Spadina or Bathurst

GOLDFISH ($$)

The facade is glass and you'll find a minimalist chic interior with a menu to match: the flavors of southeast Asia, the sub-stance of Italian pasta and a vegetarian culture.
➕ H2 ✉ 372 Bloor Street West ☎ 416/513-0077 ⏰ Lunch Wed–Sun; dinner daily 🚇 Bathurst

JOSO'S ($$)

www.josos.com
The best place for fresh fish in Toronto. Select your own fish from the tray and it will be grilled, steamed, poached, or cooked in any way to please your palate. The calamari are legendary.
➕ Off map at L1 ✉ 202 Davenport Road (just east of Avenue Road) ☎ 416/925-1903 ⏰ Lunch Mon–Fri; dinner Mon–Sat 🚇 Bay 🚌 Bus 6

AGE LIMITS

The legal drinking age in Ontario is 19, and young people should be prepared to show photo ID because entry and/or alcohol service can be refused.

MORTON'S OF CHICAGO ($$$)

www.mortons.com
A steakhouse that is a cut above the rest. The menu features United States Department of Agriculture rated prime beef.
➕ K1 ✉ Park Hyatt Hotel, 4 Avenue Road ☎ 416/925-0648 ⏰ Dinner daily 🚇 Bay or Museum

OLIVE AND LEMON ($$)

Dishes are restrained yet exuberant. They include sautéed olives and lemons with fresh bread, plump grilled sardines, daily fish and meat and spaghetti and meatballs.
➕ H3 ✉ 119 Harbor Street ☎ 416/923-3188 ⏰ Dinner daily 🚇 Spadina

SOUTHERN ACCENT ($)

www.southernaccent.com
In Markham Village, with a canopy-covered brick patio. Gumbo, jambalaya, blackened fish and other Louisiana dishes.
➕ G2 ✉ 595 Markham Street ☎ 416/536-3211 ⏰ Dinner Tue–Sun 🚇 Bathurst

TRUFFLES ($$$$)

Probably one of the best restaurants in North America. The cuisine is fresh, unusual and flavor-ful, the interior is in simple but luxurious taste.
➕ K1 ✉ Four Seasons Hotel, 21 Avenue Road ☎ 416/964-0411 ⏰ Dinner Tue–Sat 🚇 Bay

It is worth discovering some of the excellent attractions of the Greater Toronto area and beyond. You will find first-class culture, delightful and lively heritage towns and one of the greatest wonders of the natural world.

Kortright Centre
for Conservation

McMichael
Collection

Canada's
Wonderland

Maple

RUTHERFORD ROAD

RICHMOND
HILL

Richmond
Hill

LANGSTAFF ROAD

Don
Valley

VAUGHAN

Highway 7

WOODBRIDGE

407 TOLL HIGHWAY

THORNHILL

STEELES   AVENUE

Humber
Valley
Park

Black Creek
Pioneer Village

FINCH AVENUE WEST

Ross Lord
Park

Old
Cummer

York

SHEPPARD AVENUE

NORTH YORK

Don
Valley

Downsview
Park

Earl Bales
Park

Oriole

Etobicoke
North

WILSON AVENUE

401

Weston

LAWRENCE AVENUE WEST

Edwards
Gardens

African
Lion Safari

Sunnybrook
Park

ETOBICOKE

EGLINTON AVENUE WEST

YORK

Ontario
Science
Centre

Smythe
Park

ST CLAIR AVENUE WEST

Todmorden
Mills

Humber
Valley
Park

Bloor

BLOOR   STREET   WEST

EAST YORK

High Park &
Colborne Lodge

TORONTO

Kipling

QUEEN STREET WEST

QUEEN STREET EA

QEW

Exhibition

Toronto Central
Station

Mimico

Humber
Bay

GARDINER EXPRESSWAY

Humber
Bay Park

Western
Beaches

LAKESHORE

Long
Branch
Park

Toronto Island
Airport

Toronto
Harbour

Leslie
Street Spit

Toronto
Islands

Tommy
Thompson
Park

Lake Ontario

0   5 km

0   3 mile

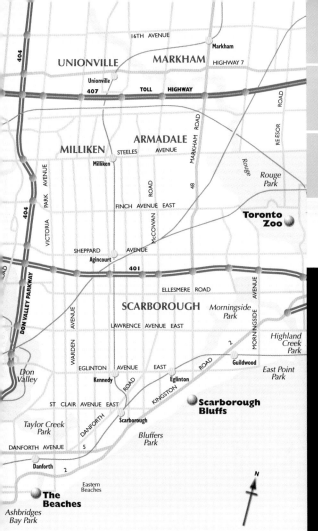

16TH AVENUE

UNIONVILLE

Markham

MARKHAM

HIGHWAY 7

404

Unionville

407   TOLL   HIGHWAY

REESOR   ROAD

ARMADALE

MILLIKEN   STEELES   AVENUE

MARKHAM ROAD

Milliken

Rouge

48

Rouge Park

VICTORIA PARK AVENUE

PARK AVENUE

ROAD

FINCH   AVENUE   EAST

404

McCOWAN

Toronto Zoo

SHEPPARD   AVENUE

Agincourt

401

DON VALLEY PARKWAY

ELLESMERE   ROAD

AVENUE

SCARBOROUGH   *Morningside Park*

LAWRENCE   AVENUE   EAST

WARDEN   AVENUE

MORNINGSIDE

Highland Creek Park

2

EGLINTON   AVENUE   EAST

ROAD

Guildwood

East Point Park

Don Valley

Kennedy

KENNEDY ROAD

Eglinton

ST   CLAIR   AVENUE   EAST

KINGSTON

Scarborough Bluffs

Taylor Creek Park

DANFORTH

Scarborough

DANFORTH   AVENUE   5

Bluffers Park

Danforth   2

Eastern Beaches

N

The Beaches

Ashbridges Bay Park

Lake Ontario

Black Creek Pioneer Village

Weaving demonstration (left); a general store (right)

THE BASICS

www.blackcreek.ca

➕ Off map to northwest

✉ 1000 Murray Ross Parkway, North York

☎ 416/736-1733

🕐 May–Jun Mon–Fri 9.30–4, Sat–Sun 11–5; Jul–Sep Mon–Fri 10–5, Sat–Sun 11–5; Oct–Dec Mon–Fri 9.30–4, Sat–Sun 11.30–4.30. Closed Jan–Apr

🍴 Restaurant

🚇 Jane subway and 35 bus; Finch subway and 60 bus

♿ Few

💷 Moderate

HIGHLIGHTS

● Coopering
● Tinsmithing
● Flour milling
● Pioneer gardens
● Laskay Emporium and post office
● Half Way House

This living-history park re-creates 19th-century Ontario village life as authentically as possible. Leave behind the stresses of modern times and step back into the past to find out about existence in a pioneer community.

Family farm Black Creek is built around the Stong family farm—their first log house (1816), smokehouse and barn (1825), and a second clapboard home that they built in 1832. Even the sheep and hogs are imported English breeds that would have been familiar to the 19th-century pioneers.

Village life The village consists of some 40 mid-19th-century buildings. Seeds are sold at the Laskay Emporium store, along with old-fashioned candy and brooms made in the village. Half Way House (it stood halfway between York and Scarborough) is a stagecoach tavern. Loaves are baked here daily in the old hearth oven. These surroundings are brought to life by the artisans who take delight in passing on their skills and knowledge. The cooper hunches over the barrel stove compressing staves to make watertight barrels and pails held together without a single nail. Others demonstrate tinsmithing, weaving, cabinet-making, blacksmithing, clockmaking and printing. Dickson's Hill School is a one-room schoolhouse that has separate entrances for boys and girls. The gardens include a herb garden with 42 familiar herbs, the weaver's dye garden with plants like bloodroot (red), sunflowers (yellow) and woad (blue), and the doctor's medicinal garden.

The cafeteria and exterior of the building housing the collection

McMichael Collection

Tom Thomson and the artists known as the Group of Seven took their easels north and painted what they saw, revealing the northern wilderness to the rest of the world. Their revolutionary works are now displayed in a woodland setting.

Artist by artist The permanent collection chronicles the development of the Group of Seven. The works of each artist are hung together so that viewers can see how the individuals evolved. All the favorites are here: the brilliantly colored canvases of Lake Superior by Alexander Young Jackson; Algonquin Park as seen by Tom Thomson; the rural villages depicted by Alfred Joseph Casson; the Killarney Provincial Park rendered by Franklin Carmichael; the starkly beautiful icebergs captured by Lawren Harris; portraits of British Columbia by Frederick Horsman Varley; and the portrayal of northwestern forests and Native Canadian villages by Emily Carr. In one gallery, a series of paintings portrays the Seven working outdoors. The most appealing depicts Franklin Carmichael sketching at Grace Lake in 1935, perching in front of an easel wrapped in a heavy parka.

First Nations and Inuit art Paintings, drawings, prints and sculptures by contemporary Native American and Inuit artists—Norval Morrisseau, Daphne Odjig, Alex Janvier, Bill Reid—are displayed in changing shows drawn from the gallery's permanent collection. Fine Inuit sculptures and other crafts complete this excellent collection.

THE BASICS

www.mcmichael.com
✚ Off map to northwest
✉ 10365 Islington Avenue, Kleinburg
☎ 905/893-1121 or 1-888/213-1121
🕐 Daily 10–4
🍴 Cafeteria
♿ Good
💷 Moderate
❓ Weekend tours at 1.30pm; special exhibition 12.30, 1.30 and 2.30

HIGHLIGHTS

- Emily Carr's *Corner of Kitwancool Village*
- Lawren Harris's *Mt. Lefroy*
- J. E. H. MacDonald's *Forest Wilderness*
- A. Y. Jackson's *First Snow*
- Tom Thomson's *Wood Interior, Winter*
- Arthur Lismer's *Bright Land*
- F. H. Varley's *Night Ferry*
- First Nations art
- Inuit sculpture

Canada's Wonderland

TOP 25

HIGHLIGHTS

- Behemoth
- Splash Works
- White Water Canyon
- The Italian Job
- Halloween events

TIPS

- Buying tickets online is cheaper; the two-day pass is a good value, and late afternoon admission is almost half price.
- You can't picnic inside the park, but there's an area outside the front gate.

Roller-coaster riders revel in this park, for it contains 15 coasters. The park has more than 65 rides and 200 attractions—adding new thrillers every year to keep the locals coming back.

Gut-wrenchers New for 2008 is Behemoth, the longest (1,616m/5,300ft), fastest (125kph/78mph) and highest (70.1m/230ft) roller coaster in Canada, with open-air seating giving terrifyingly clear views of the twists and turns, horizontal loops and eight extreme drops. Shockwave spins and loops riders through 360 degrees and 21m (70ft) into the air. The daredevil Drop Zone takes riders 70m (230ft) up and then drops them in a 96kph (60mph) free fall. The Xtreme Skyflyer lifts you to 45m (150ft) and then delivers the thrills of skydiving and hang-gliding. But the roller coasters

Clockwise from left: children meet Dora the Explorer characters; the free fall Dropzone ride; the Psyclone ride in full swing; the waterpark area of Wonderland, Splashworks; the Votex ride twists and turns over the water; the Italian Job stunt track roller coaster

remain the favorites: the looping inverted Top Gun, a standing loop version called Sky Rider, a wooden coaster, and the Italian Job stunt track.

Water plus Splashworks is the 8ha (20-acre) water park, with an extra-large wave pool generating white caps, and 18 water slides, including one with a 120m (400ft) drop in the dark. There's also a wacky aquatic jungle gym for small children.

Gentler fun There are lots of gentler rides, including an antique carousel, and young children have plenty of fun in Kidzville, Hanna-Barbera Land and Nickelodeon Central. There's also a SpongeBob SquarePants 3-D motion simulator movie. Live shows include Endless Summer (on ice), Twistin' to the 60s, Dora's Sing-A-Long Adventure and a couple of acrobatic/high dive shows.

THE BASICS

www.canadaswonderland.com

☐ Off map to northwest

✉ 9580 Jane Street Vaughan. Take Hwy 400 to Rutherford Road

☎ 905/832-7000

🕐 Early May–early Oct daily. Hours vary throughout the season

🍴 Many outlets

🚇 Yorkdale or York Mills and then GO bus

🚌 165A

♿ Few

💵 Expensive (One Price Passport). Additional fees for some events

Ontario Science Centre

- Human Body Hall
- Science Arcade
- Living Earth
- Space Hall
- TELUSCAPE
- KidSpark
- Cloud

- Look for staff wearing lab coats—they are there to help and explain.
- You save money on combined tickets if you decide to see an IMAX movie.

This leading interactive science museum designs and builds exhibits for others around the world. The museum has completed a major upgrade, with inspirational new installations. There are engaging displays for all ages.

New areas TELUSCAPE, an outdoor area in the center's forecourt, connects science to nature and the landscape with plenty of interactive exhibits. The central FUNtain enables you to make music by interrupting the water flow. Designed with teens and young adults in mind, the Weston Family Innovation Centre provides "experiences" rather than exhibits, challenging young people to look at things differently and develop their skills, from making unusual music and art to learning how to read the body language of a liar. KidSpark

provides similar fun for the under-8s, with water play, learning math and nutrition while shopping, music and art exhibits and other activities.

Old favorites The Science Arcade is where you'll find the popular hair-raising electricity demonstration, the distorted room, pedal power and puzzles and illusions. Living Earth has a re-created rain forest and other wonders, while the Human Body hall includes seeing how you'll look when you are older. The Sport hall combines athletic activities with virtual sport experiences.

Omnimax The Omnimax Theatre has a 24m (79ft) dome screen with digital wraparound sound that creates the illusion of being right in the movie. You sit in a tilted-back seat and watch a screen 10 times larger than most IMAX formats.

THE BASICS

www.ontarioscience
centre.ca
⊞ Off map to northeast
✉ 770 Don Mills Road,
North York at Eglinton
☎ 416/696-1000 or
1-888/696-1110
🕐 Daily 10–5
🍴 Food court, café, kiosks
🚇 Pape then bus 25
north; Eglinton then bus
34 east
♿ Very good
💷 Expensive

Toronto Zoo

This polar bear and gorilla are among the 5,000 animals housed at the zoo

THE BASICS

www.torontozoo.com
- Off map to northeast
- 361A Old Finch Avenue, Scarborough
- 416/392-5929
- May–end Aug daily 9–7.30; Mar–Apr, Sep–end Oct daily 9–6; Oct–end Feb daily 9.30–4.30
- Various outlets
- Kennedy and then Scarborough bus 86A going east
- Very good
- Expensive
- "Meet the Keeper" program at various times and venues throughout the day

HIGHLIGHTS

- Canadian Domain
- Eurasia Outdoor Exhibits
- Americas Pavilion
- Re-created Maya temple
- Africa Pavilion

The 5,000 or so animals here representing more than 460 species, have more freedom than many in similar institutions. Even their pavilions re-create their natural environment as much as possible.

Australasia, Eurasia and the Americas Inspired by the San Diego Zoo, the 287ha (710 acres) are organized around eight pavilions and outdoor paddocks. Inside each pavilion, habitats and climates are replicated using flora, fauna, birds and butterflies. The Australasia Pavilion is being redeveloped, and will include a new 7m (23ft) long Great Barrier Reef tank, circular column tanks for jelly fish and other sea creatures, and an Outback area. The nearby Eurasia Outdoor Exhibits include the Siberian tiger, snow leopard and yak. Frighteners in the Americas Pavilion include alligators, black widow spiders, boa constrictors, Mojave desert sidewinders and pink-toed tarantulas. A new Tundra exhibit for polar bears opens in 2009.

Africa and the Indo-Malayan Pavilion The Africa Pavilion houses the Gorilla Rainforest exhibit. Outdoors, you can go on safari observing zebra, lion, giraffe, ostrich, cheetah, hyena, elephants, white rhinos and antelope. The orangutan and white-handed gibbon entertain in the Indo-Malaya Pavilion, along with hornbill and reticulated python. Near the pavilion are the Sumatran tigers, Indian rhinoceros, lion-tailed macaque and, in the Malayan Woods Pavilion, clouded leopard. In the Canadian Domain are a large herd of wood bison plus grizzly bear, wolf and cougar.

More to See

AFRICAN LION SAFARI

www.lionsafari.com

It's not just lions here. More than 1,000 animals are kept in spacious drive-through reserves, including rhinos, primates, giraffes, zebras and elephants. There are boat and train rides, elephant bathing and birds of prey flying demonstrations and a jungle playground and wet play area.

🔁 Off map to southwest ✉ 1386 Cooper Road, Flamborough. Take Hwy 401 to Hwy 6 south ☎ 519/623-2620 🕔 Early May–late Jun Mon–Fri 9–4, Sat–Sun 9–5; late Jun–early Sep daily 9–5.30; early Sep–early Oct daily 9–4 🍴 Cafeteria/snack bar 💲 Expensive

THE BEACHES

At the eastern end of Queen Street, this is the district favored by baby boomers, attracted to the small-town atmosphere, the boardwalk along the lake and attractive Victorian homes along tree-shaded streets. Quirky stores, restaurants, cafés and antiques stores add interest.

🔁 Off map to east 🚇 Queen Street East streetcar

EDWARDS GARDENS

This garden is popular in good weather, especially its rhododendrons.

🔁 Off map to northeast ✉ Lawrence Avenue and Leslie Street ☎ 416/392-8188 🕔 Daily dawn–dusk 🚇 Eglinton then Lawrence East bus 54, 54A ♿ Good 💲 Free

HIGH PARK & COLBORNE LODGE

Colborne Lodge (1836–37) and the surrounding 161ha (400 acres) were donated to the city in 1873. Thus High Park, with a small zoo and adventure playground, was born. People come to cycle, jog, stroll, picnic, swim in the pool and use the sports fields. In winter Grenadier Pond is a skating rink.

🔁 Off map to west ✉ Bloor Street West and Parkside Drive ☎ 416/392-1111, 416/392-6916 Colborne Lodge 🕔 Colborne Lodge: daily dawn–dusk. High Park: May–Aug Tue–Sun 12–5; Sep Sat–Sun 12–5; Oct–Dec Tue–Sun 12–4; mid-Jan to Apr Fri–Sun 12–4 🚇 High Park 🚇 No. 501 streetcar ♿ Good; Colborne Lodge none 💲 Park: free; Colborne Lodge: inexpensive

Giraffes and zebras examine a visitor to the African Lion Safari

Playing volleyball at The Beaches

KORTRIGHT CENTRE FOR CONSERVATION

www.trca.on.ca

The Kortright Centre is an environmental facility, where the Power Trip Trail threads for 1.6 km (1 mile) between demonstrations on energy efficiency, renewable energy and sustainable building methods. More information can be gleaned from various projects on-site. You can enjoy more than 16 km (10 miles) of hiking trails through forest and marshland.

🚫 Off map to northwest ✉ 9550 Pine Valley Drive, Woodbridge ☎ 416/661-6600 🕐 Mon–Fri 9–4, Sat–Sun 10–4 🍴 Café 🚻 Good 💲 Inexpensive

SCARBOROUGH BLUFFS

The dramatic Scarborough Bluffs line a 14km (8.5 mile) stretch of lakeshore to the east of Toronto, where erosion has created cliffs rising to more than 60m (197ft). One of the best spots to view the cliffs is from Bluffers Park, where there's a good beach, picnic areas, a restaurant and boat ramps.

🚫 Off map to northeast

TODMORDEN MILLS

The old buildings of a mill established in the late 18th century now tell the story of Toronto's early industrial history. You can explore the former homes of the millers and see the old Don train station, the Brewery Gallery and the Paper Mill Gallery.

🚫 Off map to northeast ✉ 67 Pottery Road ☎ 416/396-2819 🕐 Apr–May Wed–Fri 12–4.30, Sat–Sun 12–5; Jun–Aug Tue–Fri 10–4.30, Sat–Sun 12–5; Sep–Dec Wed–Fri 12–4.30, Sat–Sun 12–4; Jan–Mar call for details 🚇 Broadview, then northbound buses to Mortimer Avenue 🚻 Few 💲 Inexpensive

TOMMY THOMPSON PARK

On a man-made spit of land that curves out into the lake, this area has been colonized by muskrats, woodchucks, foxes and coyotes, snakes, turtles and toads and around 45 bird species.

🚫 Off map to south ✉ Off south end of Leslie Street ☎ 416/661-6600 🕐 Apr–Oct Sat–Sun 9–6; Nov–Mar Sat–Sun 9–4.30 🚌 97B 🚻 Good 💲 Free

Bluffers Park Marina at the base of Scarborough Bluffs

Cannon outside Colborne Lodge

Excursions

KLEINBURG

Picturesque Kleinburg, on a wooded ridge above the Humber River, is a 19th-century heritage town full of lovely restored homes, specialty stores and galleries.

The Kleinburg Nashville Historical Collection, open on summer weekends, displays artifacts and photographs of the town. The big event of the year is the annual Binder Twine Festival, dating back to the days when farmers would come to town at harvest time to buy twine for their sheaves. It still has an old-time feel, with traditional crafts, and entertainment, and the highlight is the choosing of the Binder Twine Queen. The McMichael Collection is also in Kleinburg (▷ 97).

(▷ 97)

THE BASICS

www.city.vaughan.on.ca/
tourism/index.cfm

➕ Off map

🚆 GO train from Union
station to Malton, then
Bolton bus

MIDLAND

On the southern shore of beautiful Georgian Bay, this summer vacation hub is clustered around the harbor, and a short downtown tour reveals 34 huge historic murals on the walls of business premises. The most remarkable, 60m (200ft) across by 25m (80ft) high, covers a grain elevator on the harborfront.

Midland is also home to the only Canadian national shrine outside Quebec, the Martyr's Shrine, commemorating eight Jesuit missionaries who lived among the local Huron tribe for 10 years until they were slaughtered by the Iroquois. The fortified mission, Sainte-Marie Among the Hurons, has been re-created on its original site opposite the shrine. Contained within a wooden palisade, it includes a church, homes, workshops and barracks, all brought to life by costumed staff. On the edge of Little Lake, the Huronia Museum has a reconstructed typical Huron village. From the European settlement there are military artifacts, furniture and art collections. Other attractions include the Wye Marsh Wildlife Centre and cruises around the thousands of islands in Georgian Bay.

THE BASICS

www.southerngeorgianbay.
on.ca

➕ Off map

ℹ️ 208 King Street

☎ 705/526-7884

Martyr's Shrine
www.martyrs-shrine.com

✉️ East on Highway 12

☎ 705/526-3788

🕐 May–Oct daily 9–7.30

Sainte-Marie Among the Hurons
www.saintemarieamong
thehurons.on.ca

✉️ East on Highway 12

☎ 705/526-7838

🕐 May–early Oct daily
10–5; Mon–Fri only in Apr
and later Oct 🖐 Moderate

Huronia Museum
www.huroniamuseum.com

✉️ 549 Little Lake Park

☎ 705/526-2844

FARTHER AFIELD

EXCURSIONS

NIAGARA FALLS

This natural wonder of the world is on most visitors' itineraries. The Canadian side of the falls gives a far superior view to the American and though the town is marred by kitschy commercial outlets, nothing can detract from the breathtaking sight of the falls.

The best way to appreciate the power of the falls is to stand at the very top, on Table Rock, at the point where a dark green mass of water silently slithers into the abyss. It is totally mesmerizing, if rather wet. When you can tear yourself away, descend about 50m (164ft) by elevator to the two outdoor observation decks directly behind the falls. Here, more than anywhere, you can appreciate the tremendous power of the falling water.

Don't miss the *Maid of the Mist* boat ride, which departs from the bottom of Clifton Hill. You board in calm waters (and don the waterproofs provided), then voyage right into the horseshoe and the turmoil of water at the foot of the falls, venturing just a little bit farther than seems sensible. Soaked by the incredible spray, you can look up at the huge wall of water plummeting down on three sides—Niagara means "thundering water."

A little way downstream, a bend in the river forms a huge whirlpool, and you can view it from above by riding the historic cable car or from below on one of the thrilling jet-boat rides. There is also the White Water Walk, a boardwalk right at the edge of the rapids. About 8km (5 miles) north along the Niagara Parkway is the Niagara Parks Botanical Gardens, which includes a butterfly conservatory. The 56km (35 mile) Niagara Parkway winds along the Niagara River from Chippawa to Niagara-on-the-Lake past orchards, wineries, parks and picnic areas—a joy for biking and hiking.

THE BASICS

www.niagarafallstourism.com

Distance: 130km (81 miles)
Journey Time: 1 hour 30 mins

🚍 Public Transit Greyhound
☎ 416/594-1311
🛈 5400 Robinson Street
☎ 905/356-6061

The Niagara Parks Commission

www.niagaraparks.com
✉ Welcome Centres: Table Rock Centre; Murray Street; Clifton Hill at Falls Avenue; *Maid of the Mist* ticket booth
☎ 905/356-2241

Royal York

Toronto's accommodations range from budget hostels and modest bed-and-breakfasts to temples of luxury. Wherever you stay, the renowned Canadian welcome is going to make a lasting impression.

Where to Stay

Introduction

Toronto has some of the finest and most innovative hotels in the world, and staying downtown can be more picturesque than in many other cities. Here, the modern high-rises might have spectacular views over the lake, while modest bed-and-breakfasts will probably be in superbly restored heritage homes on leafy residential streets surprisingly close to the center.

Be prepared

The city has more than 35,000 hotel rooms, and it is possible to just show up and find a room—even, perhaps, a last-minute deal on the price. That said, it's usually better to arrive with a reservation. The city can fill up when one of the major festivals is on, and advance online prices are often a lot lower than for walk-ins. If you do show up without a reservation, try the Travellers' Aid Society of Toronto (www.travellersaid.ca). It has desks at the airport (tel 905/676-2868), the downtown bus terminal (tel 416/596-8647) and Union Station (tel 416/366-7788). The booths are open daily 9.30–9.30.

Hidden costs

Be aware that quoted room rates may not include local taxes: 5 percent hotel tax and 5 percent GST. There used to be tax refunds on GST for foreign visitors, but this scheme was abolished in 2007. If you arrive by car, some downtown hotels with parking garages will charge a daily parking fee and others may charge for valet parking.

HOME AWAY FROM HOME

If you are a family or group and staying for a week or more, it might be worth looking for a vacation rental—even couples can save money this way. Using the properties to full capacity, you could get a per person nightly rate of as little as $30 and make further savings by cooking for yourselves. Try visiting www.vacation-rentals411.com or www.perfectplaces.com.

Budget Hotels

PRICES

Expect to pay under $150 for a double room per night in a budget hotel.

312 SEATON

www.312seaton.com
Friendly bed-and-breakfast in Cabbagetown. Two rooms have private bathrooms; all have high-speed internet.
➕ P4 ✉ 312 Seaton Street ☎ 416/968-0775 or 1-866/968-0775; fax 416/924-8656 🚋 College streetcar

ALAN GARDENS B&B

www.alan-gardens-bandb-toronto.ca
On a tree-lined street with three cozy rooms offering luxury fabrics, TV and internet. Bathrooms are not all en suite.
➕ N5 ✉ 106A Pembroke Street ☎ 416/967-9614 or 1-800/215-1937 🚋 Dundas East streetcar

AMBASSADOR INN

www.ambassadorinntoronto.com
Ten-minutes' walk from the Eaton Centre, this stylish 1899 mansion has 20 guest rooms, all with private bathroom and most with Jacuzzi tubs.
➕ N4 ✉ 280 Jarvis Street ☎ 416/260-2608; fax 416/260-1219 🚇 College

CLARION HOTEL AND SUITES, SELBY

www.hotelselby.com
In a handsome Victorian building, this relaxed midtown hotel is good value. Suites have Jacuzzi, fireplace or sunroom. Nearby health club (fee).
➕ N2 ✉ 592 Sherbourne ☎ 416/921-3142; fax 416/923-3177 🚇 Sherbourne

FEATHERS B&B

Close to Casa Loma and the University, this is a delightful little place with just two guest rooms.
➕ H1 ✉ 132 Wells Street ☎ 416/534-1923; fax 416/534-2388 🚇 Bathurst

DORMS AND HOSTELS

In summer, university dorms provide fine budget accommodations. **Neill Wycik** (➕ N4 ✉ 96 Gerrard Street East ☎ 416/977-2320 or 1-800/268-4358, fax 977-2809), **Victoria University** (➕ J6 ✉ 140 Charles Street West ☎ 416/ 585-4522; fax 585-4530) and **University of Toronto New College** (➕ J3 ✉ 40 Willcocks Street ☎ 416/946-0529, fax: 416/ 946-3801; www.torontores. com) are all downtown, the latter on the main St. George campus. There are comfortable rooms and decent facilities (TV lounge, kitchen and laundry). **Global Village Backpackers** (✉ 460 King Street West ☎ 416/703-8540, fax 416/703-3887; www.globalbackpackers.com) is Toronto's largest travelers' hostel, with 200 beds, just a five-minute walk from The CN Tower.

HOTEL VICTORIA

www.hotelvictoria-toronto.com
In the financial district, with only 56 small rooms. Some have coffeemakers and mini-refrigerators.
➕ M7 ✉ 56 Yonge Street ☎ 416/363-1666 or 1-800/363-8228; fax 416/363-7327 🚇 King

HOWARD JOHNSON'S INN, YORKVILLE

www.hojo.com
Great location and a good value with very reasonably priced modern rooms (there are only 71, so make a reservation). No additional facilities.
➕ L1 ✉ 89 Avenue Road ☎ 416/964-1220; fax 416/964-8692 🚇 Bay or St. George

STRATHCONA

www.thestrathconahotel.com
Decent, if small, rooms at a fraction of the price of the Royal York right opposite. Coffee shop/restaurant and sports bar. 200 rooms.
➕ L7 ✉ 60 York Street ☎ 416/363-3321; fax 416/363-4679 🚇 Union

TOWN INN SUITES

www.towninn.com
Great value, spacious suites with kitchen and separate living room close to Yorkville. Facilities include swimming pool, sauna, WiFi and buffet breakfasts. Only the largest suites are beyond budget price.
➕ M2 ✉ 620 Church Street ☎ 416/964-3311 or 1-800/387-2755 🚇 Bloor/Yonge

Mid-Range Hotels

PRICES

Expect to pay between $150 and $299 per night for a double room in a mid-range hotel.

COMFORT SUITES CITY CENTRE
www.choicehotels.ca
Convenient for all downtown attractions, this is an all-suite hotel with swimming pool, fitness room and free buffet breakfast.
➕ N5 ✉ 200 Dundas Street East ☎ 416/362-7700; fax 416/362-7706 🚇 Dundas 🚋 Dundas Street East streetcar

DELTA CHELSEA
www.deltahotels.com
Large (1,591 rooms) but well-run, with excellent facilities for children.
➕ M4 ✉ 33 Gerrard Street West ☎ 416/595-1975 or 1-800/243-5732; fax 416/585-4375 🚇 College

DELTA TORONTO EAST
www.deltahotels.com
Modern hotel in Scarborough. Large pool with waterslides, saunas and fitness room, plus supervised kids' center.
➕ Off map to east ✉ 2035 Kennedy Road, Scarborough ☎ 416/299-1500 or 1-800/663-3386; fax 416/299-8959 🚇 Kennedy, then bus 43

FOUR POINTS BY SHERATON
www.starwoodhotels.com
In a great lakeshore location, west of High Park, this hotel is about 10km (6 miles) from downtown hub. It has 152 comfortable, modern rooms and a fitness facility.
➕ Off map to west ✉ 1926 Lakeshore Boulevard West ☎ 416/766-4392 🚇 Mimico 🚌 501, 508

HILTON TORONTO
www.hilton.com
Near the Convention Center; 601 rooms over 32 floors. There is an indoor/outdoor pool.
➕ L6 ✉ 145 Richmond Street West ☎ 416/869-3456; fax 416/869-0291 🚇 Osgoode

HOLIDAY INN MIDTOWN
www.holidayinn.com
A modern hotel, with fairly standard Holiday Inn rooms, but in a good spot for visiting Yorkville and the Royal Ontario Museum.
➕ J2 ✉ 280 Bloor Street West ☎ 416/968-0010 or 0800/911-617; fax 416/968-7765 🚇 St. George

BED-AND-BREAKFAST

Several bed-and-breakfast organizations help visitors to find rooms in private homes from $99 to $150 a night.
Toronto City Bed & Breakfasts
www.torontocitybandb.com
BBCanada
www.bbcanada.com

ISABELLA HOTEL & SUITES
www.isabellahotel.com
A historic and visual landmark, consisting of an 1891 mansion and 1914 seven-story tower, renovated and turned into a boutique hotel.
➕ N2 ✉ 556 Sherbourne Street ☎ 416/922-2203; fax 416/922-2204 🚇 Bloor/Yonge or Wellesley

MADISON MANOR BOUTIQUE HOTEL
www.madisonavenuepub.com
Nicely restored Victorian home with traditional furnishings in the 23 bedrooms, some of which have fireplaces. All have en suite bathrooms.
➕ J1 ✉ 20 Madison Avenue ☎ 416/922-5579 or 1-877/561-7048; fax 416/963-4325 🚇 Spadina

MAKING WAVES BOATEL
www.makingwaves-charters.com
A unique B&B, on an elegant converted trawler, with four state rooms, lounge, galley kitchen and covered deck. June to end of September only.
➕ D9 ✉ Ontario Place Marina ☎ 416/722-0379 🚌 509, 511 to Exhibition 🚉 Exhibition

METROPOLITAN
www.metropolitan.com
A challenger to the Four Seasons in terms of its restaurants, which are celebrated for their cuisine and character; service is less splendid.

The 425 modern rooms are equipped with the latest technology.
⊞ L5 ✉ 108 Chestnut Street ☎ 416/977-5000; fax 416/977-9513 Ⓜ St. Patrick

POSH DIGS II
www.poshdigs.ca
On a leafy street just off the Little Italy strip, this is a fine Victorian house with three bright, contemporary guest suites, complete with full kitchens and separate bedrooms.
⊞ G3 ✉ 414 Markham Street ☎ 416/964-6390; fax 416/922-6390 Ⓜ Ulster Street streetcar

RADISSON PLAZA HOTEL ADMIRAL
www.radisson.com/torontoca_admiral
Harborfront hotel with rooftop pool, bar and terrace. The 157 rooms are well furnished and equipped. Fitness center, two restaurants and a bar.
⊞ K9 ✉ 249 Queen's Quay West ☎ 416/203-3333 or 1-888/201-1718; fax 416/203-3100 Ⓜ Union then LRT

RENAISSANCE TORONTO DOWNTOWN
www.renaissancehotels.com
Out of 346 functional rooms, 70 overlook the Rogers Centre baseball turf. Pool, fitness center and squash courts.
⊞ J8 ✉ 1 Blue Jays Way ☎ 416/341-7100 or 1-866/237-1512; fax 416/341-5091 Ⓜ Union

RESIDENCE INN
www.marriott.com
An all-suite hotel close to the Entertainment District and Rogers Centre. Each suite has a full kitchen and lots of amenities. Some have great views.
⊞ J7 ✉ 255 Wellington Street West ☎ 416/581-1800; fax 416/581-0255 Ⓜ St. Andrew

SHERATON
www.sheratoncentretoronto.com
One of the city's largest

hotels (1,377 rooms), with efficient service. Six restaurants/bars.
⊞ L6 ✉ 123 Queen Street West ☎ 416/361-1000 or 1-866/716-8101; fax 416/947-4801 Ⓜ Osgoode

SUITES AT 1 KING WEST
www.onekingwest.com
Stunning contemporary suites and a health club in a landmark high-rise hotel. It incorporates the historic former banking hall of the Toronto Dominion Bank.
⊞ M7 ✉ 1 King Street West ☎ 1-866/470-5464 Ⓜ King Ⓜ King Street West streetcar

WESTIN BRISTOL PLACE
www.starwoodhotels.com
One of the best hotels on the airport strip. The 287 rooms are well furnished and equipped. Pools and fitness facilities.
⊞ Off map to northwest ✉ 950 Dixon Road ☎ 416/675-9444; fax 416/675-4426 Ⓜ Kipling

WESTIN PRINCE
www.starwoodhotels.com
Set in 6ha (15 acres), 20 minutes from downtown in the Don Valley. The 381 rooms are serene. Katsura restaurant has excellent sushi and robata bars, tempura counter and teppanyaki-style cuisine. Putting green, tennis courts and fitness center.
⊞ Off map to northeast ✉ 900 York Mills Road, Don Mills ☎ 416/444-2511 Ⓜ York Mills

THE COOLEST ROOMS
Hotel Le Germain (⊞ J/K7 ✉ 30 Mercer Street ☎ 416/345-9500) is a member of a small, very chic and modern Montréal chain. A bowl of green apples highlights the front desk and a fireplace warms the minimalist modern lobby-lounge.
The Drake Hotel (⊞ D6 ✉ 1150 Queen Street West ☎ 416/531-5042) is in a run-down, but gentrifying part of the city and attracts a hip clientele to its "crash pads," which are small but "ultra designed."
The Soho Metropolitan Hotel (⊞ J7 ✉ 318 Wellington Street West ☎ 416/599-8800) is the sister of the Metropolitan Hotel and has similar contemporary luxe style right down to the Dale Chihuly artwork and the top-class restaurant, Senses.

Luxury Hotels

PRICES

Expect to pay more than $300 per night for a double room at a luxury hotel.

FAIRMONT ROYAL YORK

www.fairmont.com
Rooms vary and the service can be stretched as there are 1,365 rooms. Nine bars and restaurants—the Library Bar is noted for its martinis. Pool.

➕ L7 ✉ 100 Front Street West ☎ 416/368-2511 or 1/800-257-7544 (reservations only); fax 416/368-9040 Ⓡ Union

FOUR SEASONS

www.fourseasons.com
In the heart of Yorkville, this is the city's top hotel. The service is personal yet unobtrusive, the 380 rooms spacious, elegant, comfortable and well equipped, and the facilities excellent. It has a world-class restaurant, Truffles (▷ 92), a great bar, Avenue (▷ 90), and the Studio Café attracts a celebrity crowd.

➕ K1 ✉ 21 Avenue Road ☎ 416/964-0411; fax 416/964-2301 Ⓡ Bay

HAZELTON HOTEL

www.thehazeltonhotel.com
Opened in 2007, this fabulous hotel has huge rooms and suites providing the ultimate luxury, from granite bathrooms to in-room entertainment

centers. There's also a fine-dining restaurant, spa and movie screening room.

➕ L1 ✉ 118 Yorkville Avenue ☎ 416/963-6300, 1-866/473-6301; fax 416/963-6399 Ⓜ Bloor/Yonge or Museum

MARRIOTT EATON CENTRE

www.marriotteatoncentre.com
Conveniently located, this renovated hotel has 459 luxurious rooms with high-tech amenities such as big-screen TV, a rooftop pool and four restaurants and lounges.

➕ L5 ✉ 525 Bay Street ☎ 416/597-9200 or 1-800/905-0667; fax 416/597-9211 Ⓡ Dundas

COUNTRY LUXURY

For a languorous country-house experience convenient for the attractive Victorian town of Stratford, book a room at **Langdon Hall**. Built in 1902, it stands in 81ha (200 acres) with superb accommodations set around a cloister garden. The main house has a lovely dining room and conservatory. Facilities include outdoor pool, tennis court, croquet lawn, billiards room, spa-fitness center and cross-country ski trails.

✉ 1 Langdon Drive, Cambridge, ON N3H 4R8 ☎ 519/740-2100; fax 519/740-8161; www.langdonhall.ca

PARK HYATT

http://parktoronto.hyatt.com
The 346 rooms have been renovated to an exceptional standard with fine fabrics and furnishings and the latest amenities. There are two restaurants—the chic, international bistro, Annona, and the Roof Lounge, serving bar meals—and a still-water spa.

➕ K2 ✉ 4 Avenue Road ☎ 416/925-1234; fax 416/924-4933 Ⓡ Bay or Museum

ROYAL MERIDIEN KING EDWARD

www.starwoodhotels.com
An architectural jewel in marble and sculpted stucco. The Café Victoria is a favorite gathering place. The 261 rooms are very spacious, well decorated and equipped.

➕ M7 ✉ 37 King Street East ☎ 416/863-9700; fax 416/367-5515 Ⓡ King

WESTIN HARBOUR CASTLE

www.starwoodhotels.com
Large 38-story hotel in a lakefront location handy for the CN Tower, Air Canada Centre, and the Entertainment and Financial districts; many of the 977 rooms have a lake view. The excellent facilities include Toula, for fine Italian dining, squash and tennis courts and an indoor pool.

➕ M9 ✉ 1 Harbour Square ☎ 416/869-1600; fax 416/869-0573 Ⓡ Union

Here is the key information to smooth your path both before you go and when you arrive. Get savvy with the local transportation, explore Toronto, or check out what festivals are taking place.

Planning Ahead

When to Go

The best time to visit Toronto is in summer, when Ontario Place, Canada's Wonderland and all the other attractions are open, and the ferries to the islands are in full swing. Fall is also good. The weather is still warm, and outside the city the forests take on a rich golden glow.

TIME

Toronto is on Eastern Standard Time, 3 hours ahead of Los Angeles, and 5 hours behind GMT.

AVERAGE DAILY MAXIMUM TEMPERATURES											
JAN	FEB	MAR	APR	MAY	JUN	JUL	AUG	SEP	OCT	NOV	DEC
23°F	26°F	35°F	47°F	57°F	68°F	70°F	70°F	64°F	53°F	42°F	30°F
−4°C	−3°C	1°C	8°C	14°C	19°C	21°C	21°C	18°C	12°C	6°C	−1°C

Spring (mid-March to late May) is unpredictable. Occasional snow or ice storms occur as late as mid-April.

Summer (early June to late August) is warm to hot, with occasional rain or humidity and cooler evenings.

Fall (September and October) has cooler temperatures, sunny days and occasional rain; the weather is ideal for exploring.

Winter (November to March) can be harsh. November is always unpredictable and mid-winter is much colder because of the unrelenting winds blowing off Lake Ontario.

SPORTING CALENDAR

Athletics
Toronto Waterfront Marathon: late Sep;
Toronto Marathon: mid-Oct

Baseball
Toronto Blue Jays, Rogers Centre: Apr–Oct

Basketball
Toronto Raptors, Air Canada Centre: Oct–Apr

Football
Toronto Argonauts, Rogers Centre: Jun–Oct
Championship games: Grey Cup (national), Vanier Cup (university) and Metro Bowl (high school): all late Nov

Hockey
Toronto Maple Leafs, Air Canada Centre: Oct–Apr
Toronto Marlies, Ricoh Coliseum, Exhibition Place: Oct–Apr

Horse racing
Queen's Plate Woodbine Racetrack: late Jun

Lacrosse
Toronto Rock, Air Canada Centre (2008 season cancelled)

Motor Racing
Steelback Grand Prix of Toronto. Exhibition Place: early Jul

Soccer
Toronto Lynx and Lady Lynx, Centennial Park Stadium, Etobicoke: May–Jul
Toronto Football Club, National Soccer Stadium, Exhibition Place: Apr–Oct

Water sports
Dragon Boat Festival, Toronto Islands: mid-Jun
Great White North Dragon Boat Race, Western Beaches Watercourse, Marilyn Bell Park: early Sep

Toronto Online

www.torontotourism.com
Toronto's official tourist website is run by
the Toronto Visitors and Convention Bureau.
Shopping, accommodations, attractions,
theater and restaurants.

www.toronto.com
A comprehensive Toronto guide. Good event
and concert listings, shopping information, plus
excellent links.

www.toronto.ca
The City of Toronto's comprehensive attractions guide, with history and archive photos.

www.where.ca/toronto
Practical info and up-to-date event listings.

www.thestar.com and **www.torontolife.com**
Two good media sites with listings.

www.ontariotravel.net
The Ontario's official travel information site.

www.niagarafallstourism.com
Niagara Tourism's official site.

www.niagaraparks.com
Niagara region tourist information, focusing on
accommodations and attractions.

www.goliveto.ca and **http://tapa.ca**
Toronto Alliance for the Performing Arts sites
listing all the theater, dance, ballet, opera, comedy and musical theater companies in Toronto;
links to box offices and ticket agencies.

www.toronto.ca/ttc
Toronto Transit Commission site, with details
about buses, subways and streetcars.

www.findtheway.ca
Information about transit systems for the city
and outlying areas.

GOOD TRAVEL SITES

www.fodors.com
A complete travel-planning
site. Reserve air tickets, cars
and rooms; research prices
and weather; pose questions
to fellow travelers; and find
links to other sites.

www.worldweb.com
A comprehensive travel
guide. Plan your trip aided
by online hotel reservation,
info about transportation,
weather, restaurants, events;
and shopping. Maps and
photo gallery.

CYBERCAFÉS

Toronto Reference Library
The best place to go online.
The banks of computers can
be used for long or short
periods.
✉ 789 Yonge Street
☎ 416/395-5577
🕐 Mon–Thu 9.30–8.30,
Fri 9.30–5.30, Sat 9–5
💵 Free

Internet Centre
✉ 324 Yonge Street
☎ 416/408-0400
🕐 8am–1am
💵 $3 per hour

JoyNet on Bloor
✉ 322 Bloor Street West
☎ 416/324-8596
🕐 Mon–Sat 9am–midnight,
Sun 10am–midnight
💵 $2 per 30 minutes

Getting There

ENTRY REQUIREMENTS

Citizens of EU and most British Commonwealth countries require a valid passport and return or onward ticket but no visa. New regulations to be imposed by the US Department of Homeland Security are expected to stipulate that US citizens returning from abroad (including Canada) by land, sea or air will need to show a valid passport or other documents as determined by the Department. The new rules come into force as early as January 2008. People under 18 must have a parent or guardian letter stating a length of stay. If children are traveling with a divorced parent who shares custody, that parent must carry the legal custody documents. If children are traveling with adults who are not parents or guardians, those adults must carry the written permission of the parents or guardians.

AIRPORT

Pearson International Airport lies northwest of Toronto, about 27km (17 miles) from the city center. A $4.5 billion redevelopment of the airport was completed in 2007, providing an, efficient and environmentally friendly Terminal 1.

Pearson International Airport

Toronto

48km (30 miles)
32km (20 miles)
16km (10 miles)

ARRIVING BY AIR

For Pearson International Airport ☎ Terminal 1: 416/247-7678; Terminal 2: 416/247-7678; Terminal 3: 416/776-5100. Approved airport taxis and limos to greater Toronto leave from the arrivals level of each terminal. Fare is determined by zone; arrange it in advance with the dispatcher or driver. To downtown the cost is $40–$50. Journey time is usually 30–40 minutes. The Airport Rocket (Bus 192) operates a daily service between around 5.30am and 2am to Kipling Station, Dundas Street and East Mall Crescent. The journey time is approximately 20 minutes. The 58A Malton route operates daily from 5am to 1am from the airport to Lawrence West Station, with a journey time of around an hour. Passengers arriving during the night can get the 300A Bloor-Danforth route (about 45 minutes to Yonge and Bloor) or the 307 to Yonge and Eglinton (about 45 minutes). Both night services run half-hourly. The single-journey ticket price for all of these services is $2.75. For further information, contact the Toronto Transit Commission (TTC ☎ 416/393-4636 and select option 7; www.toronto.ca/ttc). In addition, GO Transit has an hourly bus to

York Mills and Yorkdale train stations (from Terminal 1 only). It runs from 6am to 1am Mon–Sat and 9am–1am Sun and takes about a half-hour to Yorkdale and 45 minutes to York Mills (☎ 416/869-3200; www.gotransit.com).

ARRIVING BY BUS
Greyhound Canada (☎ 416/367-1465; 800/661-8747) and commuter buses arrive at the Metro Coach Terminal (☎ 416/393-7911) at 610 Bay Street near Dundas, in easy reach of Dundas and St. Patrick subway stations.

ARRIVING BY CAR
The US highway system leads directly into Canada. From Michigan, you enter at Detroit-Windsor via I-75 and the Ambassador Bridge or Port Huron-Sarnia via I-94 and the Bluewater Bridge. From New York State, using I-90 you can enter at Buffalo-Fort Erie; Niagara Falls, NY-Niagara Falls; or Niagara Falls, NY-Lewiston. Using I-81, you can cross at Hill Island; using Route 37, you cross either at Ogdensburg-Johnstown or Rooseveltown-Cornwall. Once across the border, you approach Toronto from the west by the Queen Elizabeth Way or Highway 401, from the east by Highway 2 or Highway 401. You need your driver's license, car registration and proof of car insurance. Boston is 896km (557 miles) from Toronto; Buffalo 169km (105 miles); Chicago 838km (521 miles); New York 801km (498 miles). Visitors entering from the US should check the latest information on travel documentation before leaving home. The US is planning to impose passport requirements for all travelers (including US citizens) using land and sea crossings between Canada and the US (▷ panel, 116).

ARRIVING BY TRAIN
Amtrak (☎ 800/872-7245 in the US) and VIA Rail (☎ 888/842-7245; www.viarail.ca in Canada) long-distance trains arrive at Union Station, which is linked directly to the subway.

INSURANCE
Make sure your policy covers accidents, medical expenses, personal liability, trip cancellation and interruption, delayed departure and loss or theft of personal property. If you plan to rent a car, check your insurance covers you for collision, personal accident liability and theft or loss.

CUSTOMS REGULATIONS
● Visitors over 18 may bring in free of duty up to 50 cigars, 200 cigarettes and 200 grams of tobacco; 1.5 liters of spirits or wine may be imported by travelers over the minimum drinking age of the province to be visited (19 in Ontario).
● No firearms, plants or meats may be imported.
● Information from Canadian Border Services Agency ☎ 506/636-5064; www.cbsa.gc.ca

Getting Around

DRIVING IN TORONTO

The city speed limit is 30mph (48kph), and right turns at red lights are permitted unless posted otherwise, but pedestrians on crosswalks have priority. Seat belts are compulsory. Towing is among the parking penalties. Call TripInfo (☎ 416/599-9090) for details of road closures.

VISITORS WITH A DISABILITY

Currently 28 subway stations are accessible, with more planned. Accessible buses run on 103 routes in Toronto, though not all the stops will be accessible. Those that are have the wheelchair symbol on the post. Visit the TTC website (www.toronto.ca/ttc). Wheel-Trans offers a door-to-door service (6am–1am) for registered customers (☎ 416/393-4111, 416/393-4311 for hearing impaired). Parking privileges are extended to drivers who have disabled plates or a pass allowing parking in "No Parking" zones. Many buildings are barrier-free and well equipped with elevators. For more information, contact Community Information Centre of Metropolitan Toronto ✉ 425 Adelaide Street West, 2nd floor, Toronto, ON M5V 3C1 ☎ 416/397-4636 ◉ Daily 8am–10pm.

Toronto has an excellent and reliable public transportation network, comprising subway, buses and streetcars.

SUBWAY, STREETCARS AND BUSES

● The subway is fast, quiet, clean and easy to use.

● The subway consists of two major lines, Bloor–Danforth and Yonge–University–Spadina. The first runs east–west from Kipling Avenue in the west to Kennedy Road in the east, where it connects with Scarborough Rapid Transit. The second runs from Finch Avenue in the north to Union Station, where it loops north along University Avenue connecting with the Bloor Line at St. George before proceeding to Downsview Avenue. There is also a short line connecting Sheppard and Don Mills. Construction of an extension of the Yonge and Spadina subway lines is due to start soon, with completion anticipated in 2015.

● You need a token (5 for $11.25, 10 for $22.50 or single fare $2.75), which can be bought in any subway station. Drop it into the box at the ticket window or into the turnstile. Day, weekly and monthly passes are available. A day pass ($9) covers one adult from the start of service until 5.30am the next day, for unlimited travel on all regular TTC routes. On weekends and statutory holidays, the same ticket will cover a family: either two adults, or two adults and up to four children 19 or under, or one adult and up to 5 children aged 19 or under. The weekly pass costs $32.25 ($25.50 for students and senior citizens); the monthly Metropass costs $109 ($91.25 for students and senior citizens).

● Discounts are available for students aged 19 and under, senior citizens and children under 12.

● The subway system is connected to the bus and streetcar network. It is always wise to pick up a transfer at the subway station from the red push-button machine at the entrance or from the bus driver. By so doing, you can board a streetcar going east or west from the subway

station if you need to, or transfer from the bus to the subway without paying extra. Transfers are only available for continuation of a journey, and can't be used if you stopover in between.

● If you are not transferring, a bus ride costs a token, or you can pay with the exact change.

● Bus stops are at or near corners and are marked by elongated signs with red stripes and bus and streetcar diagrams. Pick up a Ride Guide map at subway stations.

● Be warned—bus stops are not always easy to see.

● The subway operates Mon–Fri 6am–1.30am and Sun 9am–1.30am. A Blue Night Network is in operation outside those hours on basic surface routes, running about every 30 minutes. Blue reflective bands indicate the bus stops served.

● From Union Station a Light Rapid Transit (LRT) line operates to Harbourfront, stopping between Queen's Quay and Rees Street. No transfer is needed to ride the LRT.

● For transit information pick up a Ride Guide, available at subway stations, tourist offices and other public places, or call ☎ 416/393-4636 (7am–10pm).

TAXIS

● Cabs can be hailed on the street.

● The light on the rooftop will be turned on if the taxi is available.

● All taxis must display rates and contain a meter.

● Tip 15–20 percent.

● If you need to call for a cab, these are some of the options:

Beck Taxi ☎ 416/751-5555
City Taxi ☎ 416/241-1400 or 1-888/494-8294
Co-op Cabs ☎ 416/504-2667
Crown Taxi ☎ 416/292-1212 or 416/750-7878
Diamond Taxicab ☎ 416/366-6868

These, and a number of other companies, can also be reached via a connection service, ☎ 416/TAXICAB.

VISITOR INFORMATION

You can obtain information from: **Tourism Toronto** ✉ 207 Queen's Quay West, Suite 590, in the Queen's Quay Terminal ☎ 416/203-2600 or 800/499-2514 @ Mon–Fri 9–5. The visitor information center in the Atrium on Bay is open daily.

WOMEN ALONE

Women traveling alone on buses at night (9pm–5am) can request to get off between stops to be closer to their destination. If you require this service, let the driver know at least one stop before you want to get off. You will get off at the front, and rear bus doors are kept closed to prevent a fellow passenger from following.

Essential Facts

NATIONAL HOLIDAYS

New Year's Day (January 1)
Good Friday and/or Easter Monday
Victoria Day (third Monday in May)
Canada Day (July 1)
Civic Holiday (first Monday in August)
Labour Day (first Monday in September)
Thanksgiving (second Monday in October)
Remembrance Day (November 11)
Christmas Day (December 25)
Boxing Day (December 26)

MONEY

The Canadian dollar is the unit of currency (= 100 cents). Coins include 1¢ (penny), 10¢ (dime) and 25¢ (quarter), and $1 (loonie) and $2 (twoonie). Bills are $5, $10, $20, $50 and $100. Stores may refuse large bills.

5 Canadian dollars

10 Canadian dollars

20 Canadian dollars

50 Canadian dollars

ELECTRICITY
● 110v, 60Hz AC. US-style flat 2-pin plugs.

MEDICAL AND DENTAL TREATMENT
● 24-hour emergency service is provided by the Toronto General Hospital ☎ 416/340-4800. The main entrance is at 200 Elizabeth Street, another entrance is at 150 Gerrard Street West.
● If you need a doctor, ask at your hotel or seek a referral from the College of Physicians and Surgeons ✉ 80 College Street ☎ 416/967-2600 🕐 9–5
● In the event of a dental emergency ask for a referral from the Ontario Dental Association ☎ 416/922-3900

MEDICINES
● Always bring a prescription for any medications in case of loss and also to show to the customs officers if necessary.
● Shopper's Drug Mart (✉ 465 Yonge Street ☎ 416/408-4000) stays open 24 hours. Pharma Plus (✉ 68 Wellesley Street at Church ☎ 416/924-7769) is also open until midnight.

MONEY MATTERS
● Most banks have ATMs that are linked to Cirrus, Plus or other networks and this is the easiest way to secure cash. Check that your PIN is valid in Canada. Also check on frequency and amount limits of withdrawals. For ATM locations visit www.mastercard.com for MasterCard and for Visa/Plus, www.visa.com.
● Credit cards are widely accepted. American Express, Diner's Club, Discover, MasterCard and Visa are the most common.
● Traveler's checks are accepted in all but small shops as long as the denominations are low ($20 or $50). If you carry traveler's checks in Canadian dollars, you save on conversion fees.

OPENING HOURS
● Banks: Mon–Fri 9 or 9.30–4 or 5pm; some are open longer and some open Sat with reduced hours.

● Museums: hours vary.

● Shops: generally Mon–Wed 9.30 or 10–6, Sat, Sun 10–5. Hours are often extended on Thu or Fri until 8 or 9. Malls stay open later.

POST OFFICES

● Postal services can be found at convenience and drugstores. Look for a sign in the window advertising postal services.

● There are also post office windows open in major shopping complexes like Atrium on the Bay ➕ L5–M5 ☎ 416/506-0911; Commerce Court ➕ L7–M7 ☎ 416/956-7452; Toronto Dominion Centre ➕ L7 ☎ 416/360-7105; First Canadian Place ➕ L7 ☎ 416/364-0540

SMOKING

● Smoking is banned in all public buildings, except in clearly designated smoking areas. All bars and restaurants are nonsmoking zones.

TAXES

● The provincial retail sales tax (PST) is 8 percent; there is also a 5 percent tax on hotel/motel rooms and a national goods and services tax (GST) of 5 percent.

● Note that GST and PST are added to purchases at the till, which can make price-tag prices seem more of a bargain that they are.

● Nonresidents can no longer apply for a refund of taxes.

TELEPHONES

● To dial outside the Toronto area codes of 416 or 905 add the prefix 1.

● To avoid hotel surcharges on local calls use a payphone. Some hotels offer free local calls.

● For long distance use AT&T, MCI or Sprint rather than calling direct. Access codes and instructions are found on your phone card. If they don't work, dial the operator and ask for the access code in Canada.

● To call the UK from Toronto dial 01144 and drop the first "0" from the number. To call the US from Toronto dial 1 plus the area code.

EMERGENCY NUMBERS

Fire, police, ambulance
☎ 911
Metro police station
✉ 40 College Street
☎ 416/808-2222
Rape Crisis
☎ 416/597-8808
Victim Services
☎ 416/808-7066
Lost property: For articles left on a bus, streetcar or subway, TTC Lost Articles Office ✉ Bay Street subway station ☎ 416/393-4100
🕐 Mon–Fri 8–5. If you lose a credit card or traveler's checks, report the loss immediately to the credit card company or the company issuing the checks, and to the local police.
All embassies are in the national capital Ottawa. The following consulates are found in Toronto:
UK ✉ 777 Bay Street at College ☎ 416/593-1290
Australia ☎ 175 Bloor Street East ☎ 416/323-1155
USA ☎ 360 University Avenue ☎ 416/595-1700

Festivals and Events

FILM FESTIVALS

Toronto and the movies have become inseparable, with "Hollywood North" attracting the biggest names to the city's studios and locations. A whole clutch of festivals showcases the new releases and recognizes the artistic contribution of those who made and starred in them. The Toronto International Film Festival in September is one of the most important film festivals in the world and the city is full of international celebrities. 2008 is its 33rd year, and around 350 movies will be screened. The Toronto International Film Festival for Children in April shows intelligent movies for kids, and other festivals include the Hot Docs Canadian International Documentary Festival (April); the Toronto Jewish Film Festival, and the Inside Out Toronto Lesbian and Gay Film and Video Festival (both in May); and the Italian Film Festival and Worldwide Short Film Festival (both in June).

JANUARY/FEBRUARY

WinterCity Festival Canadian and international musicians give open-air performances, plus indoor happenings including restaurant events. *Late Jan/early Feb.*

MARCH

Canadian Music Week For four days hundreds of bands play venues all over the city. Also a music industry conference, trade show and awards gala events. *Early Mar.*

St. Patrick's Day One of the largest paddy parades in the world starts at noon on Bloor Street (at St. George). *Nearest Sun to Mar 17.*

APRIL

National Home Show The Direct Energy Centre at Exhibition Place hosts a showcase of homes and interiors. *Early/mid-Apr.*

MAY

Santé—The Bloor-Yorkville Wine Festival Toronto's most upscale shopping area hosts this celebration of the finest international wines, with gourmet food events. *Early May.*

JUNE

Luminato Festival A 10-day arts festival with music, dance, film, literature, theater and visual arts. Various venues. *Early Jun.*

Distillery Blues Festival Three days of free concerts featuring the best blues performers, with two stages. *Mid-Jun.*

North by Northeast Toronto rocks with 500 bands in 40 venues, plus music movies, big-name speakers and related events. *Mid-Jun.*

Pride Toronto and Gay Pride Parade The city's arts and culture festival celebrating diverse gender identities. *Mid-Jun.*

Toronto Downtown Jazz Festival A 10-day event showcasing the finest Canadian and international musicians. *Mid/late Jun.*

Festival of Fire Four (nonconsecutive) nights of spectacular fireworks choreographed to music. At Ontario Place. *Late Jun/early Jul.*

JULY

Canada Day Open-air concerts, fireworks and other events. *Jul 1.*

The Toronto Fringe Festival An eclectic mix of theatrical events. *Early Jul.*

Caribana—Toronto Caribbean Carnival The city sways to the sounds of calypso, reggae, steel bands and soca. Ontario Place, Exhibition Place and other venues. *Early Jul/mid-Aug.*

AUGUST

Toronto's Festival of Beer Around 200 brews from across the country. *Mid-Aug.*

Canadian National Exhibition and Air Show Three-day air show. Exhibition Place. *Mid-Aug/early Sep.*

SEPTEMBER

Virgin Fest A two-day music festival on the Islands with four stages (Smashing Pumpkins, Bjork, The Killers in 2007). *Early Aug.*

The Word on the Street National literary festival featuring readings, storytelling events and other events in various venues. *Late Sep.*

OCTOBER

Toronto International Art Fair One of the finest and most comprehensive art events in Canada. *Late Oct.*

International Bach Festival Various venues. *Late Oct/early Nov.*

NOVEMBER

Canadian Aboriginal Festival and Canadian Aboriginal Music Awards A huge First Nations celebration at the Rogers Centre with food, art and crafts, and music. *Mid-Nov.*

Cavalcade of Lights Christmas begins with the switch-on of 100,000 lights. *Late Nov.*

DECEMBER

Tafelmusik's Sing-Along Messiah Fun Christmas event at Massey Hall. *Dec 23.*

CityTV New Year's Eve Nathan Phillips Square is packed with revelers. *Dec 31.*

CULTURAL FEASTS

In this multicultural city, there are a number of excellent festivals relating to the various "old countries" and they provide a great way to learn about the cultures that are being kept alive—not to mention the wonderful food. They include the colorful Chinese New Year in Chinatown (Jan/Feb); Taste of Little Italy, based around College Street (Euclid to Shaw), in mid-June; Taste of the Danforth, celebrating Greektown and its food and culture in mid-August; the Festival of South Asia, on Gerrard Street East (Coxwell to Greenwood) in mid-August and the same neighborhood's Diwali celebration in mid-November; Bloor West Village Ukrainian Festival at the Harbourfront and the Hispanic Fiesta on Mel Lastman Square, Yonge Street, both from late August to early September; Roncesvalles Village Polish Festival, in the village in west Toronto, in mid-September.

Timeline

REBELLION

The first mayor of Toronto, William Lyon Mackenzie, shared immigrant aspirations for political reform and campaigned vehemently against the narrow-minded, exclusive power of the Family Compact—a group of ardent British loyalists who controlled the city's economy and politics. By 1837 he was advocating open rebellion, and on December 5 around 700 rebels assembled at Montgomery's Tavern. Led by Mackenzie, they marched on the city. The sheriff called out the militia, who scattered the rebels at Carlton Street. Mackenzie fled to the United States. Two other ringleaders were hanged.

Left to right: a polished stone Inuit carving in the Inuit Gallery; an ornate Inuit mask in the Bay of Spirits Gallery; an ancient Inuit painting, The Shaman's Wife, in the Kleinsburg Museum

1715 Fort Rouille is built.

1720 France sets up a trading post at Toronto.

1763 The Treaty of Paris secures Canada for Britain.

1787 The British purchase land from the Mississauga tribe on which Toronto will be sited.

1793 John Graves Simcoe, Governor of Upper Canada, arrives and names settlement York.

1813 Americans invade, destroy Fort York, and burn Parliament Buildings.

1834 The city is named Toronto ("meeting place"). William Lyon Mackenzie becomes the first mayor.

1837 Former mayor, Mackenzie, leads rebellion against the Family Compact (▷ panel).

1844 George Brown founds The Globe.

1858 The Toronto Islands are created from a peninsula smashed by a violent storm.

1867 Canadian Confederation: Toronto becomes capital of Ontario province.

1884 The streets are lit by electricity.

1914–18 70,000 Torontonians enlist and 13,000 are killed in World War I.

1920 The Group of Seven hold their first art exhibition.

1923 The Chinese Exclusion Act restricts Chinese immigration.

1933 The Depression leads to 30 percent unemployment.

1950 Sunday sports are permitted.

1953 Metro plans under way.

1992/3 Blue Jays win the World Series.

1995 The Conservative Government is elected and focuses on budget cuts.

1996 *Fortune* magazine names Toronto "Best City for Work and Family outside the US."

1998 Toronto's six municipalities merge.

2002/3 Toronto Transit's new Sheppard Line connects the former city of North York to downtown.

2003 Distillery Historic District opens.

2007 A 10-year, multibillion dollar redevelopment of Toronto Pearson International Airport is completed.

BUILDING TORONTO

1844 First City Hall
1845 King's College
1851 St. Lawrence Hall
1852 The Toronto Stock Exchange
1869 Eaton's
1886 The Provincial Parliament buildings
1907 The Royal Alexander
1912 The Royal Ontario Museum
1931 Maple Leaf Gardens arena
1965 New City Hall
1971 Ontario Place
1972 Harbourfront development
1975 CN Tower
1989 SkyDome stadium
1993 CBC Building
2006 Four Seasons Centre for the Performing Arts
2007 Michael Lee-Chin Crystal at ROM
2008 Art Gallery of Ontario redevelopment

An interpreter in 19th-century British military uniform in the grounds of Fort York (left); exhibit of stone age hunters in the Royal Ontario Museum (right)

Index

INDEX

CITYPACK TOP 25
Toronto

WRITTEN BY Marilyn Wood
ADDITIONAL WRITING Penny Phenix
DESIGN CONCEPT Kate Harling
COVER DESIGN AND DESIGN WORK Jacqueline Bailey
INDEXER Marie Lorimer
IMAGE RETOUCHING AND REPRO Michael Moody, Sarah Montgomery
EDITOR Bookwork Creative Associates Ltd
SERIES EDITORS Paul Mitchell, Edith Summerhayes

© **AUTOMOBILE ASSOCIATION DEVELOPMENTS LIMITED 2008**

First published 1997
Colour separation by Keenes, Andover
Printed and bound by Leo Paper Products, China

A CIP catalogue record for this book is available from the British Library.

ISBN 978-0-7495-5709-6

Published by AA Publishing, a trading name of Automobile Association Developments Limited, whose registered office is Fanum House, Basing View, Basingstoke, Hampshire RG21 4EA. Registered number 1878835.

A03145
Mapping in this title produced from map data supplied by Global Mapping, Brackley, UK. Copyright © Global Mapping/ITMB
Transport map © Communicarta Ltd, UK

The Automobile Association wishes to thank the following photographers, companies and picture libraries for their assistance in the preparation of this book.

Abbreviations for the picture credits are as follows – (t) top; (b) bottom; (c) centre; (l) left; (r) right; (AA) AA World Travel Library.

Front cover AA/J F Pin; **back cover (i)** AA/N Sumner; **(ii)** AA/C Sawyer; **(iii)** AA/N Sumner; **(iv)** AA/N Sumner; **1** AA/J Davison; **2** AA/N Sumner; **3** AA/N Sumner; **4t** AA/N Sumner; **4c** AA/N Sumner; **5t** AA/N Sumner; **5c** AA/N Sumner; **6t** AA/N Sumner; **6cl** AA/J Davison; **6c** AA/N Sumner; **6cr** Imagestate; **6bl** AA/N Sumner; **6bc** Canoe, Oliver Bonacini Restaurants; **6br** Digital Vision; **7t** AA/N Sumner; **7cl** Stockbyte; **7c** St Lawrence Market; **7cr** AA/J Davison; **7bl** AA/N Sumner; **7bc** AA/A Mockford & N Bonnetti; **7br** AA/N Sumner; **8** AA/N Sumner; **9** AA/N Sumner; **10t** AA/N Sumner; **10/11t** Tourism Toronto; **10c** AA/C Sawyer; **10/11c** AA/N Sumner; **10/11b** AA/N Sumner; **11t** AA/N Sumner; **11c** AA/N Sumner; **12t** AA/N Sumner; **12b** Photodisc; **13t** AA/N Sumner; **13ct** AA/N Sumner; **13c** AA/N Sumner; **13b** AA/N Sumner; **14t** AA/N Sumner; **14ct** AA/N Sumner; **14c** AA/P Enticknap; **14cb** AA/N Sumner; **14b** AA/N Sumner; **15t** AA/N Sumner; **15b** Photodisc; **16t** AA/N Sumner; **16ct** Canoe, Oliver Bonacini Restaurants; **16c** AA/J Davison; **16cb** The Distillery District; **16b** The Distillery District; **17t** AA/N Sumner; **17ct** Tourism Toronto; **17c** AA/J Davison; **17cb** The Legislative Assembly of Ontario; **17b** AA/N Sumner; **18t** AA/N Sumner; **18ct** The Distillery District; **18c** Digital Vision; **18bl** AA/N Sumner; **18br** Photodisc; **19t** AA/N Sumner; **19ct** AA/J Davison; **19c** AA/N Sumner; **19cb** AA/J Davison; **19b** AA/N Sumner; **20/21** J F Pin; **24** Tourism Toronto; **24/25t** AA/N Sumner; **24/25c** AA/N Sumner; **25cl** AA/N Sumner; **26l** AA/N Sumner; **26tr** AA/N Sumner; **26/27** AA/J Davison; **27t** AA/N Sumner; **27cl** AA/N Sumner; **27cr** AA/N Sumner; **28l** AA/J Davison; **28/29t** AA/N Sumner; **28/29c** AA/J Davison; **29cl** AA/J Davison; **29cr** AA/J Davison; **30l** AA/N Sumner; **30c** AA/N Sumner; **30r** AA/N Sumner; **31l** Museum of Contemporary Canadian Art; **31r** Installation view of the exhibition Unholy Alliance: art + fashion meet again, Museum of Contemporary Canadian Art, photo by Walter Willems; **32l** AA/J F Pin; **32r** AA/J F Pin; **33t** AA/N Sumner; **33br** AA/J Davison; **33bl** AA/N Sumner; **34** AA/N Sumner; **35** AA/N Sumner; **36** AA/N Sumner; **37** AA/N Sumner; **38** AA/N Sumner; **39** AA/C Saywer; **40** AA/C Sawyer; **41** AA/N Sumner; **44** AA/N Sumner; **44/45t** AA/N Sumner; **44/45c** AA/N Sumner; **45cl** AA/N Sumner; **45cr** AA/N Sumner; **46** Design Exchange; **47t** Design Exchange; **47cl** Design Exchange; **47cr** Design Exchange; **48** The Distillery District; **49t** The Distillery District; **49cl** The Distillery District; **49cr** The Distillery District; **50l** AA/J Davison; **50r** AA/J Davison; **51l** St Lawrence Hall; **51r** St Lawrence Hall; **52t** AA/N Sumner; **52bl** Tourism Toronto; **52br** AA/N Sumner; **53t** AA/N Sumner; **53bl** Festival hat, China, late 19th to early 20th century, gift of Fred Braida, T85.0704 Textile Museum of Canada; **53br** Kimono, Japan, early 20th century, gift of Wendy Wright T99.20.1 Textile Museum of Canada; **54** Tourism Toronto; **55** AA/N Sumner; **56** AA/N Sumner; **57** AA/C Sawyer; **58** AA/C Sawyer; **59** AA/N Sumner; **62l** AA/N Sumner; **62tr** AA/N Sumner; **62/63** AA/N Sumner; **63t** AA/N Sumner; **63cl** AA/N Sumner; **63cr** AA/N Sumner; **64** AA/N Sumner; **64/65t** AA/N Sumner; **64/65c** AA/N Sumner; **65cl** AA/N Sumner; **65cr** AA/N Sumner; **66** Tourism Toronto; **66/67t** AA/J Davison; **66/67c** AA/J Davison; **67cl** AA/N Sumner; **67cr** Tourism Toronto; **68t** AA/N Sumner; **68bl** Tourism Toronto; **68br** Tourism Toronto; **69t** AA/N Sumner; **69b** Alamy (Val Dunca/Kenebec Images); **70** Tourism Toronto; **71** AA/N Sumner; **72** AA/N Sumner; **73** Brand X Pictures; **74** AA/C Sawyer; **75** Casa Loma; **78l** AA/N Sumner; **78tr** Bata Shoe Museum; **78/79** AA/J Davison; **79t** Bata Shoe Museum; **79cl** AA/J Davison; **79cr** AA/J Davison; **80l** AA/J Davison; **80r** Casa Loma; **81** Casa Loma; **82l** AA/J Davison; **82c** AA/J Davison; **82r** AA/J Davison; **83** AA/J Davison; **84l** AA/N Sumner; **84tr** Tourism Toronto; **84/85** AA/N Sumner; **85t** Tourism Toronto; **85cl** AA/J Davison; **85cr** AA/N Sumner; **86l** AA/J Davison; **86r** AA/J Davison; **87t** AA/N Sumner; **87bl** AA/J Davison; **87br** AA/J Davison; **88** AA/N Sumner; **89** AA/N Sumner; **90** AA/N Sumner; **91** Digital Vision; **92** AA/C Sawyer; **93** AA/J Davison; **96l** AA/N Sumner; **96r** AA/N Sumner; **97l** McMichael Canadian Art Collection; **97r** McMichael Canadian Art Collection; **98l** Canadian Wonderland; **98tr** Canadian Wonderland; **98cr** Canadian Wonderland; **99t** Canadian Wonderland; **99cl** Canadian Wonderland; **99cr** Canadian Wonderland; **100/101** AA/J Davison; **101** AA; **102l** AA/N Sumner; **102br** AA/N Sumner; **103t** AA/N Sumner; **103bl** African Lion Safari; **103br** AA/N Sumner; **104t** AA/N Sumner; **104bl** Tourism Toronto; **104br** AA/J Davidson; **105** AA/N Sumner; **106** AA/N Sumner; **107** AA/N Sumner; **108t** AA/C Sawyer; **108ct** Photodisc; **108c** Photodisc; **108cb** Photodisc; **108b** AA/S McBride; **109** AA/C Sawyer; **110** AA/C Sawyer; **111** AA/C Sawyer; **112** AA/C Sawyer; **113** AA/N Sumner; **114** AA/N Sumner; **115** AA/N Sumner; **116** AA/N Sumner; **117** AA/N Sumner; **118** AA/N Sumner; **119** AA/N Sumner; **120t** AA/N Sumner; **120b** MRI Bankers' Guide to Foreign Currency, Houston, USA; **121** AA/N Sumner; **122** AA/N Sumner; **123** AA/N Sumner; **124t** AA/N Sumner; **124bl** AA/J Davison; **124bc** AA/J Davison; **124br** AA/J F Pin; **125t** AA/N Sumner; **125bl** AA/J Davison; **125br** AA/J Davison

Every effort has been made to trace the copyright holders, and we apologise in advance for any unintentional omissions or errors. We would be pleased to apply any corrections in any following edition of this publication.